EASY GUIDE TO THE
BIBLE

EASY GUIDE TO THE
BIBLE

THE OLD AND NEW TESTAMENTS EXPLAINED

FALL RIVER PRESS

New York

FALL RIVER PRESS

New York

An Imprint of Sterling Publishing Co., Inc.
1166 Avenue of the Americas
New York, NY 10036

ISBN 978-1-4351-6438-3

Distributed in Canada by Sterling Publishing Co., Inc.
c/o Canadian Manda Group, 664 Annette Street
Toronto, Ontario, Canada M6S 2C8
Distributed in the United Kingdom by GMC Distribution Services
Castle Place, 166 High Street, Lewes, East Sussex, England BN7 1XU

For information about custom editions, special sales, and premium and corporate
purchases, please contact Sterling Special Sales at 800-805-5489
or specialsales@sterlingpublishing.com.

Manufactured in the United States of America

2 4 6 8 10 9 7 5 3 1

www.sterlingpublishing.com

Contents

THE OLD TESTAMENT

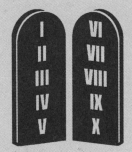

CONTENTS — THE OLD TESTAMENT

CONTEXT

THE OLD TESTAMENT IS THE FIRST, longer portion of the
Christian Bible. It is the term used by Christians to refer to
the Jewish scriptures, or Hebrew Bible. The Old Testament
is not one book written by a single author, but a collection of ancient
texts written and re-written by numerous authors and editors for
hundreds of years. They tell the story of the ancient Israelites, or
Hebrew people, and contain the laws and rituals that comprise their
religion. For Jews, the collection comprises the *Torah*—the law
for worship and everyday living—as well as the history of God's
promise to them. For Christians, the Old Testament is also sacred,
but they view its religious meaning as incomplete without the life
and teachings of Jesus Christ as related in the New Testament.
Muslims trace their religious roots to some of the figures in the
Old Testament, although they deny the religious significance of
the work as a whole. In general, the Old Testament is essential to
the way Western civilization has long thought and talked about
God, as well as ethics, justice, and the nature of the world.

In its current form, the collection of the Old Testament books
was completed by the first century B.C. The individual books
themselves, however, are much more ancient—some dating to the
tenth and eleventh centuries B.C. or earlier. Because these works
purport to tell the history of human origins, many of the events
occur much earlier and cannot be historically verified. Later
interactions between the nation of Israel and the ancient world,
however, can be verified, and historians use these dates to approx-
imate the biblical events. It is estimated that the chronology of the
Old Testament covers more than 1500 years, from approximately
2000 B.C. to 400 B.C.

The setting of the Old Testament is the ancient Near East (or Middle East), extending from Mesopotamia in the northeast (modern-day Iraq) down to the Nile River in Egypt in the southwest. The majority of the events take place in Palestine, the ancient land of Canaan—the eastern Mediterranean region stretching seventy-five miles west from the sea and marked by the Jordan River Valley, which runs down the heart of the mountainous land. Situated between the sprawling Egyptian Empire to the south and the Hittite and Babylonian Empires to the north and east, the area was an important trade route in the second millennium B.C. A variety of peoples, mostly nomadic herding communities, scattered the plains. They established small fortified cities, worshipped various deities, and farmed. The inhospitable region prevented any one nation from dominating the area, but the inhabitants were generally called "Canaanite," speaking versions of a common Semitic language, including the languages now known as Hebrew and Arabic.

Very little is known about the early existence of the Israelites outside of the biblical story. In fact, there are no references to Israel in ancient texts prior to 1200 B.C. The Old Testament explains that the Hebrew people (the term used for the Israelites by non-Israelites) were the descendants of a Semitic man named Abraham, who moved to the land of Canaan in obedience to God. Ancient references to a group of outcasts and refugees known as habiru exist, but there is little evidence to indicate that these were the Hebrew people. The biblical story tells how the Israelites suffered as slaves in Egypt for many years, and how they miraculously emigrated to Canaan, where they conquered the land and its people in a sweeping military campaign. If true, modern scholars believe this migration may refer to the thirteenth or twelfth century B.C., when a vast vast upheaval probably occurred in the urban communities of the

Canaanite region. However, it is unlikely that a violent or swift conquest by the Israelites took place. Historians believe that the Israelites may have been a part of a gradual, peaceful resettlement, or even a peasant uprising.

The glory of the Israelites in the Old Testament is the vast, united kingdom of David and his son, Solomon, who established a royal capital in Jerusalem, erected a grand temple, and expanded Israel's borders to the Euphrates River. According to the order of biblical events, David and Solomon's kingdoms probably existed around the tenth century B.C. The historical existence of such an Israelite empire is unclear; but after this point, the nation of Israel began to surface in the events of the ancient Near East. The Old Testament describes the tragic division of Israel into two kingdoms and the litany of evil kings who eventually caused the Israelites' demise at the hands of the Assyrian and Babylonian Empires. Historical evidence corroborates some of these events. The northern area of Israel was captured by the Assyrian Empire in 722–720 B.C. The southern area of Israel, called "Judah," was conquered by the Babylonian king Nebuchadnezzar, who destroyed the legendary city of Jerusalem and its temple from 589–586 B.C. A large population of Israel's upper class—including artisans, rulers, and religious leaders—were exiled and resettled in Babylonian territory.

The period of the Israelites' exile proved extremely important to the formation of Judaism as an organized religion. The Jewish community's need to retain its identity in a foreign land prompted great theological and literary developments. Much of the Old Testament, especially the religious laws and prophecy, was written whole-cloth or rewritten and edited at this time. The experience of the exile caused the Old Testament writers to define the Torah, or God's laws, and to emphasize biblical themes like suffering and the reversal of fortune. When Babylon fell to the Persian Empire in 539 B.C., the Persian king Cyrus permitted the Jews to return to their homeland. The biblical books of Ezra and Nehemiah (neither of which is discussed in this study guide) document the return of the Jews to Jerusalem under Ezra's leadership, sometime around 460–400 B.C. The impoverished Jews rebuilt Jerusalem and erected a second temple, identifying themselves as a religious community and following the laws of the Torah.

Israel's history and geography is thus crucial to an appropriate understanding of the Old Testament. The region in which the biblical events take place was an area of constant ethnic and political change. The Old Testament depicts the Israelites as a separate and enduring entity throughout this change—a race of Hebrew people descended from one man, possessing a divine right to the land, and distinguishable from the surrounding peoples by its monotheism, or worship of one god. Whether or not these claims are true, the Israelites certainly existed as a people, and the Old Testament remains one of the most vivid pictures of the historical, religious, and literary life of the ancient Near East.

As a work of literature, the Old Testament contains many literary forms, including narrative and poetry, as well as legal material and genealogies. Critics often use terms such as *epic*, *myth*, and *legend* to classify the biblical stories, as well as describing the heroes, dialogue, and symbols within the text as examples of its literary qualities. Such concepts represent modern and classical ways of understanding literature and were most likely foreign to the authors of the Old Testament. Nevertheless, the Old Testament itself greatly influenced the way Western civilization has thought about literature and stories. As a result, describing the biblical stories through literary terminology remains an important way of understanding the significance of the Old Testament as literature.

Structure and Composition

The Old Testament contains thirty-six books, three of which are separated into two volumes, rendering a total of thirty-nine individual books. The Hebrew Bible divides the books into three main categories: the Pentateuch, the Prophets, and the Writings. In addition to the Old Testament books accepted as scripture by Jews and Protestants, Catholics consider seven "deuterocanonical" books to be scripture. Because the authors of the Old Testament books are largely unknown, scholars believe that the final form of the books indicates the work of "redactors," or editors, who performed a practice common in ancient near eastern literature. The redactors combined previously existing writings, oral traditions, and folktales, and added their own material, to compose the completed books. Often, the redactors attributed a book or a group of books to a significant biblical figure to add validity to their work.

The Pentateuch (Greek for "five scrolls") comprises the first five books of the Old Testament—Genesis, Exodus, Leviticus, Numbers, and Deuteronomy. The collection of books was probably in its final form by the fourth century B.C. The Pentateuch represents the most important section of biblical narrative. It explains the origins of the human race and the rise of the Israelites, including the Israelites' miraculous emigration from Egypt. More than half of the Pentateuch is devoted to God's laws and commandments to Israel. Jews call these books the *Torah*, or law, because of its religious precepts and for the model of ethical behavior that the leading characters prescribe.

Moses, the hero of the Pentateuch, was traditionally assumed to be the work's author. However, modern scholars describe the Pentateuch as the time-worn product of four ancient writers and editors, each of whom revised and expanded existing work. Scholars label the unknown contributors "J," "E," "P," and "D," and identify "J" as the oldest writer, a scribe in King David's court. Different parts of the narrative and laws in the Pentateuch are ascribed to each contributor based on differences in the style and theology of the text.

The second category of Old Testament books comprises the Prophets. Many of these works were composed during or after Israel's exile in the sixth and fifth centuries B.C. The books can be divided into two further categories: the Former Prophets and the Latter Prophets. The Former Prophets are sometimes called the "Historical Books" because they continue the story of the Israelites from the death of Moses to the fall of Jerusalem in 587 B.C. The four works—Joshua, Judges, 1 and 2 Samuel, and 1 and 2 Kings—follow the Pentateuch in the Christian Bible. Scholars sometimes surmise that, together, these books represent the work of a single, unknown editor labeled the "Deuteronomist," who combined separate stories and added work of his own to form a coherent history of the Israelites. The Latter Prophets (which are not covered in this study guide) include the fifteen books of Isaiah, Jeremiah, Ezekiel, and twelve "Minor Prophets." Written before or during the Israelites' exile, these difficult works include sayings and oracles about Israel's downfall, its salvation from exile, and theology.

The Writings denotes the final category of the Hebrew Bible, collected in its present form around the first century B.C. Some of these books are later works chiefly concerned with Israel's history during and after the exile, such as Lamentations, Esther, Daniel, Ezra, and Nehemiah (most of which are not covered in this study guide). With the exception of Ruth and the two books of Chronicles, the remaining books—Job, Psalms, Proverbs,

Ecclesiastes, and Song of Solomon—represent the biblical books of poetry and wisdom and are placed after the Historical Books in the Christian Bible. Some are quite ancient, and many represent collections of traditional poems and sayings attributed by a later editor to King David or King Solomon.

Roman Catholic and Greek Orthodox versions of the Old Testament contain an additional category of books called the "deuterocanonical writings," or "Apocrypha." These fifteen books were included in the Septuagint, the Greek version of the Jewish scriptures translated by scribes in Alexandria, Egypt, between the third and first centuries B.C. The Apocrypha contains additional works of poetry and wisdom and, more importantly, stories about Israel during the Greek and Roman periods. These works were not included in the Hebrew Bible, but they were included in the canon, or list, of Old Testament books accepted by the early Christian church. They were later excluded from Protestant versions of the Old Testament following the Reformation in the sixteenth century A.D., and are not included in this study guide.

PLOT OVERVIEW

THE OLD TESTAMENT IS A COLLECTION of thirty-nine books about the history and religion of the people of Israel. The authors of these books are unknown, and each book possesses a unique tone, style, and message.

Individually, they include stories, laws, and sayings that are intended to function as models of religious and ethical conduct. Together—through hundreds of characters and detailed events— they represent a unified narrative about God and his attempt to relate to humankind by relating to a specific group of people.

The Old Testament contains four main sections: the Pentateuch, the Former Prophets (or Historical Books), the Writings, and the Latter Prophets. This study guide covers books from the first three sections.

THE PENTATEUCH

The Pentateuch comprises the first five books of the Old Testament. It depicts a series of beginnings—the beginning of the world, of humankind, and of God's promise to the Israelites.

Genesis, the first book, opens with God's creation of the world. The perfect world falls into evil when humans disobey God, and the human population divides into separate nations and languages. After many generations, God speaks to a man named Abraham. God makes a promise, or covenant, with Abraham to make his descendants into a great nation and to give them a great land. Abraham shows strong faith in God, and God seals his promise with a number of signs and tests. This special covenant with God passes on to Abraham's son, Isaac, and to his grandson, Jacob. Together, they represent the patriarchs, or fathers, of the Israelite people. Jacob's twelve sons move to Egypt after the youngest brother, Joseph, miraculously becomes a high official in Egypt.

In the Book of Exodus, the descendants of Jacob's children have become a vast people, but the Pharaoh of Egypt holds them in slavery. God chooses one man, Moses, to rescue the Israelites. God sends ten plagues to Egypt, and, with miraculous signs and wonders, Moses leads the people out of Egypt and across the Red Sea. They go to Mount Sinai, where God appears in a cloud of thunder over the mountain and affirms to the Israelites the promise he made to Abraham. God commands them to worship only himself, and he gives them various ethical and religious laws.

The books of Leviticus, Numbers, and Deuteronomy continue the explanation of God's religious laws and his promises to the people. The people must keep these laws to enter and enjoy the promised land, toward which they are heading. Despite God's presence, the Israelites complain and disobey incessantly, inciting God's wrath. They wander the wilderness for forty years in search of the promised land. These books continue the period of Moses's legendary leadership and miracles, until his death at the end of Deuteronomy.

THE FORMER PROPHETS

The Former Prophets, or the Historical Books, cover the history of the Israelites from Moses's death to the fall of the nation in 587 B.C. In the books of Joshua and Judges, the Israelites successfully conquer the land promised to them by God, but they disobey God by worshipping the deities of the surrounding peoples. Neighboring nations invade and oppress the Israelites. God saves the people of

Israel by designating judges, or rulers, to lead the people in warding off their enemies.

The two books of Samuel (First Samuel and Second Samuel) cover the rise of the united kingdom of Israel. Israel's religious leader, Samuel, appoints a king named Saul. Saul disobeys God, however, and God chooses another man, David, to be Israel's king. King Saul attempts to kill the young David, but fails. Saul's death closes the first book. In the second book, David establishes the great kingdom of Israel. He conquers Israel's surrounding enemies and establishes Jerusalem as the religious and political center of Israel.

The books of Kings (called 1 Kings and 2 Kings) trace the decline of Israel's success. God blesses David's son, Solomon, with immense wisdom. As king, Solomon expands Israel into an empire and builds a great temple in Jerusalem. Solomon disobeys God by worshipping other deities, and, at his death, the kingdom splits into a northern kingdom, Israel, and a southern kingdom, Judah. A host of evil kings leads the two kingdoms away from worshipping God. Despite the attempts of the prophets Elijah and Elisha to halt Israel's wrongdoing, the two kingdoms fall to the Assyrian and Babylonian Empires. Jerusalem is destroyed, and the people are sent into exile.

The Writings

The Writings are placed after the historical books in the Christian Bible. Some of these are narratives covering the time of Israel's exile in other nations and its eventual return to the homeland. The Book of Esther, for example, tells the story of an unassuming Jewish girl who becomes the queen of Persia and boldly saves the Jewish people from genocide.

THE OLD TESTAMENT

Many of the Writings are books of poetry and wisdom, among the most important literature in the Old Testament. The Book of Job is a lengthy dialogue investigating God's justice and the problem of human suffering. The Psalms are lyrical poems and hymns—many attributed to King David—that express humankind's longing for God. The books of Proverbs and Ecclesiastes—similarly attributed to the wise King Solomon—offer sayings and instructions about the meaning of life and ethical behavior. Lastly, the Song of Solomon (also attributed to Solomon) is a romantic, lyric dialogue between a young woman and her lover.

CHARACTER LIST

God　　　　The creator of the world and an all-powerful being.
God calls himself the only true deity worthy of human
worship. As the figurehead of Israel and the force
behind every event, God acts as the unseen hero of the
Old Testament. God reveals his intentions by speaking
to people. Physical manifestations of God are always
indirect or symbolic. God appears in many different
forms, including an angel, a wrestler, a burst of fire,
and a quiet whisper.

Abraham　　The patriarch of the Hebrew people. Abraham is
traditionally called "Father Abraham" because
the Israelite people and their religion descend from
him. God establishes his covenant, or promise,
with Abraham, and God develops an ongoing
relationship with the Israelites through Abraham's
descendants. Abraham practices the monotheistic
worship of God, and his resilient faith in God,
despite many challenges, sets the pattern for the
Israelite religion's view of righteousness.

Moses　　　The reluctant savior of Israel in its exodus from
Egyptian bondage to the promised land. Moses
mediates between God and the people, transforming
the Israelites from an oppressed ethnic group into a
nation founded on religious laws. Moses's legendary
miracles before Pharaoh, along with his doubts and
insecurities, make him the great mortal hero of the

Old Testament. He is the only man ever to know God "face to face." Four out of the five books of the Pentateuch are devoted to Moses and Israel's activities under his leadership.

David   The king of Israel and the founder of Jerusalem, or "Zion." David's reign marks the high point of Israel in the biblical narrative. Although David's claim to the throne is threatened by Saul and by David's own son, Absalom, David maintains his power by blending shrewd political maneuvering with a magnanimous and forgiving treatment of his enemies. David's decision to bring the Ark of the Covenant—Israel's symbol of God—to the capital of Jerusalem signals the long-awaited unification of the religious and political life of Israel in the promised land.

Jacob   The grandson of Abraham, Jacob is the third patriarch of the Israelite people and the father of the twelve sons who form the tribes of Israel. Jacob experiences a life fraught with deception, bewilderment, and change. He steals his brother Esau's inheritance right and wrestles with God on the banks of the Jabbok River. Appropriately, the nation that springs from Jacob's children derives its name from Jacob's God-given name, "Israel." "Israel" means "struggles with God," and Jacob's struggles are emblematic of the tumultuous story of the nation of Israel.

Joseph   Jacob's son and the head official for the Pharaoh of Egypt. Despite being sold into slavery by his brothers,

Joseph rises to power in Egypt and saves his family from famine. Joseph's calm and gracious response to his brothers' betrayal introduces the pattern of forgiveness and redemption that characterizes the survival of the Israelite people throughout the Old Testament.

Saul   Israel's first king. After God chooses Saul to be king, Saul loses his divine right to rule Israel by committing two religious errors. Saul acts as a character foil to David, because his plot to murder David only highlights David's mercy to Saul in return. Saul's inner turmoil over the inscrutability of God's exacting standards makes him a sympathetic but tragic figure.

Solomon   David's son and the third king of Israel. Solomon builds the opulent Temple in Jerusalem and ushers in Israel's greatest period of wealth and power. God grants Solomon immense powers of knowledge and discernment in response to Solomon's humble request for wisdom. Solomon's earthly success hinders his moral living, however, and his weakness for foreign women and their deities leads to Israel's downfall.

Elijah and Elisha   The prophets who oppose the worship of the god Baal in Israel. After the division of Israel into two kingdoms, Elijah and his successor, Elisha, represent the last great spiritual heroes before Israel's exile. Their campaign in northern Israel against King Ahab and Jezebel helps to lessen Israel's growing evil but does not restore Israel's greatness. Israel's demise makes

Elijah and Elisha frustrated doomsayers and miracle workers rather than national leaders or saviors.

Adam and Eve

The first man and woman created by God. Adam and Eve introduce human evil into the world when they eat the fruit of a tree God has forbidden them to touch.

Noah

The survivor of God's great flood. Noah obediently builds the large ark, or boat, that saves the human race and the animal kingdom from destruction. Noah is the precursor to Abraham, because Noah represents the first instance of God's attempt to form a covenant with humanity through one person.

Isaac

Abraham's son and the second member in the triumvirate of Israel's patriarchs. Isaac's importance consists less in his actions than in the way he is acted upon by others. God tests Abraham by commanding him to kill his son Isaac, and Isaac's blindness and senility allow his own son Jacob to steal Isaac's blessing and the inheritance of God's covenant.

Aaron

Moses's brother, who assists Moses in leading the Israelites out of Egypt. God designates Aaron to be the first high priest in Israel. The quiet Aaron often stands between Moses and the people to soften Moses's angry response to their sinful behavior.

Joshua

The successor of Moses as Israel's leader. Joshua directs the people in their sweeping military campaign to conquer and settle the Promised Land. Joshua's persistent exhortations to Israel to remain obedient to God imply that he doubts Israel will do so. His exhortations foreshadow Israel's future religious struggles.

Samson   One of Israel's judges and an epic hero who thwarts the neighboring Philistines with his superhuman strength. Samson is rash, belligerent, and driven by lust for foreign women—qualities that contradict Jewish religious ideals. Samson's long hair is both the source of his strength and the symbol of his religious devotion to God as a Nazirite. Samson's character demonstrates that in the bible, heroic potential is gauged not by human excellence but by faith in God.

Samuel   The last of Israel's judges and the prophet who anoints both Saul and David as king. Samuel fulfills political and priestly duties for Israel, but he ushers in Israel's monarchy mainly as a prophet—one who pronounces God's words and decisions. Samuel's stoic and aloof position in Israel allows Saul to struggle with God and his fate on his own.

Absalom   David's son, who attempts to overthrow his father's throne. Absalom's violent rise to power suggests that the evil that corrupts Israel comes from within.

Joab   King David's loyal military commander. Joab serves as a foil to David's successful combination of religion and politics. Joab's reasonable desire to see justice and retribution delivered to the kingdom's traitors emphasizes the unusual quality of David's kindness to his enemies.

Rehoboam and Jeroboam   The opposing kings who divide Israel into the northern kingdom of Israel and the southern kingdom of Judah. Rehoboam and Jeroboam introduce rampant worship of idols and false gods into their kingdoms. Each king acts both as a point of contrast and a double, or mirror, for the other, allowing the biblical reader to trace the rapid growth of evil in Israel's two kingdoms.

Ahab and Jezebel   The most wicked rulers of Israel. Ahab and Jezebel spread cult worship of the pagan god Baal throughout the northern kingdom. Dogs gather to eat their blood at their deaths, fulfilling Elijah's prophecy.

Esther   A timid Jewish girl who becomes the queen of Persia. Esther boldly and cunningly persuades the king of Persia to remove his edict calling for the death of the exiled Jews.

Job   The subject of God and Satan's cosmic experiment to measure human faithfulness to God in the midst of immense pain. Job scorns false contrition and the advice of his friends, preferring instead to question God's role in human suffering. He retains an open and inquisitive mind, remaining faithful in his refusal to curse God.

ANALYSIS OF MAJOR CHARACTERS

GOD

In the Old Testament, God is unique, sovereign, and unchanging. He differs from Greek gods, whose faults and quarrels cause events. His unchanging nature is hinted at by his names. In biblical Hebrew, God is called "YAHWEH," meaning "to be." This title is similar to the title God uses with Moses, "I AM WHO I AM." However, the God presented in Old Testament does contradict himself at times. In the course of two chapters in Exodus, God threatens to destroy the Israelites, relents, and then pronounces himself loving, forgiving, and slow to anger. God grants himself the power of self-description; he is whoever he says he is.

Each biblical writer gives God human characteristics. For example, God speaks. We do not know how his listeners recognize that it is he who is speaking or what he sounds like, but God certainly embraces the ability to articulate his intentions through the human convention of language. Also, God assumes human form. He appears as an angel, as a group of three men, and as a mysterious army commander. In a sense, God takes on human qualities like a costume that can also be taken off, since his specific appearances do not offer a complete picture of him. Still, these manifestations suggest that there is a fundamental humanity to the personality of the Hebrew God. God casually walks in the garden with Adam and Eve. He even physically wrestles Jacob and allows Jacob to beat him. These humble and endearing qualities of God contrast his later appearances as a pillar of fire and a thunderous mountain. The more extreme manifestations are, like the human manifestations, only a part of God's character rather than his sole mode of existence.

God's initial interaction with humankind is unsolicited. Noah, Abraham, and Moses do not ask God to form a relationship with them. Even when God is unseen, his immense power over human fate lurks beneath the events of the Old Testament narrative. On the surface, the characters' experiences are filled with suspense. The characters submit to chance and have a desperate, irrational faith in God. When God speaks or appears, we realize he has been in control all along, and the fear or suspense seems unfounded, trite, or comical. Amidst the gravity of human events, God's willingness to cause momentous events in order to teach a lesson shows him to be a strangely playful character.

MOSES

Moses is one of the few characters whose complete biography is described by the biblical narrative, and the early events of his life characterize him as a product of his circumstances. Born in Egypt, Moses is raised by Pharaoh's daughter, who takes pity on the abandoned Hebrew baby. After an impulsive murder, Moses flees west, where he begins a life as a shepherd and stumbles into God in the form of a burning bush. He reluctantly agrees to return to Egypt and demand the Israelites' release, but agrees to little more. Each event in the journey from Egypt to Mount Sinai, where God delivers his laws to the Israelites, propels Moses further into the roles of prophet, priest, ruler, and savior of Israel.

Moses' most heroic virtue is his steadfast obedience, and it might be said that a passive quality permeates each of his miracles. Ten plagues strike Egypt because Moses simply appears in Pharaoh's court to request the release of the Israelites. With the help of his rod, or divine staff, Moses parts the waters of the Red Sea merely by outstretching his arms. Later, the beleaguered Israelites defeat a mighty army when two men help Moses raise his hands for the duration of the battle. The image of a stationary man bringing about overwhelming physical feats is striking. Moses himself is far from passive or reticent, yet he represents a prototype of the biblical hero whose greatness lies not in self-assertion but in obedience to God.

Moses is a compelling figure because he possesses human faults. He is passionate and impulsive. Descending from Mount Sinai, Moses knows ahead of time that the people are worshipping a golden idol, because God has warned him of this fact. Upon seeing the people, Moses angrily breaks the stone tablets inscribed with God's laws. God seems to value this passionate quality in Moses, for Moses is an effective mediator between God and the Israelites. He prays with a sense of urgency, unafraid to ask God to refrain from divine retribution and willing to accept the blame for the people's actions. His earnest attention to the present situation and to God's demands earns Moses the opportunity to speak with God face to face. Yet his passion remains his weakness. God commands Moses to produce water from a rock by speaking to it, but, irritated with the people's complaints, Moses hits the rock with his staff. This act of negligence bars Moses from entering the very promised land to which he has guided the Israelites for almost half a century.

DAVID

David is a strong but unassuming shepherd who becomes God's choice to replace Saul as king of Israel. He is humble yet self-possessed, readily dismissing human opinion. His humility becomes clear early in his youth, when he kills the giant Goliath with a sling stone, declining the opportunity to use Saul's royal armor. As king, his foremost quality is obedience to God. For example, when his wife expresses embarrassment at David's dancing while he marches into Jerusalem, he rebukes her, boasting that he will embarrass himself so long as it pleases God.

David's mercy to others displays his selflessness—a product of his strenuous commitment to ethical ideals. His sense of propriety is striking when he refrains from killing Saul while Saul has his back turned. David scorns the easy opportunity to attack because he feels it would be morally wrong to strike God's current anointed ruler. As king, David forgives the kingdom's traitors, and executes the traitors of his enemies. When his own rebellious son dies, David cries aloud in public, "O my son Absalom, my son, my son Absalom!" (2 Samuel 18:33). His weeping suggests the depth of a father's blind love for his son.

David's mercy may also be interpreted as a product of his political aspirations. David refuses to kill Saul because he senses that whatever standards he imposes against the current king may one day be used against himself as ruler. Moreover, seeds of revolt have already been planted in the northern tribes of Israel by David's reign, and the kingdom's unity may be on shaky ground. King David shows mercy to his traitors, especially Absalom, because he wishes to quell emotions and court the graces of all his subjects. By this reading, David appears to be a pragmatist—one who acts not out of his or her ideals, but on the basis of what is practical or expedient. However, the Old Testament ultimately seems to suggest that David's religious ideals do not conflict with his pragmatism.

THEMES, MOTIFS, AND SYMBOLS

THEMES

Themes are the fundamental and often universal ideas explored in a literary work.

THE PROBLEM OF EVIL

The Old Testament both raises and attempts to answer the question of how God can be good and all-powerful yet allow evil to exist in the world. From Adam and Eve's first disobedient act in the garden, each biblical book affirms that human evil is the inevitable result of human disobedience, not of God's malice or neglect. The first chapters of Genesis depict God as disappointed or "grieved" by human wickedness, suggesting that the humans, rather than God, are responsible for human evil (Genesis 6:6). Later books, such as Judges and Kings, show God's repeated attempts to sway the Israelites from the effects of their evil. These stories emphasize the human capacity to reject God's help, implying that the responsibility for evil lies with humanity. Judges echoes with the ominous phrase, "The Israelites again did what was evil in the sight of the Lord . . ." (Judges 3:12).

The most troublesome challenge to God's goodness, however, is the existence of natural evil, which is the undeserved destruction and pain humans often experience. God repeatedly instructs the Israelites to destroy entire cities, killing men, women, and children in the process. The Book of Job directly questions God's implication in natural evil. God punishes Job harshly for no other reason than to prove to Satan that Job is religiously faithful. In the end, God declares to Job that God's powerful ways are beyond human understanding and should not be questioned. The book implies that God sometimes uses natural evil as a rhetorical device—as a means of displaying his power or of proving a point in a world already tainted by human corruption.

THE POSSIBILITY OF REDEMPTION

God typically responds to human behavior with retributive justice, meaning that people get what they deserve. God punishes the evil and blesses the righteous. The theme of mercy and redemption, which develops throughout the biblical stories, contrasts with this standard of retribution.

Redemption appears in two forms in the Old Testament. Sometimes, one person forgives another by simply forgetting or ignoring the other's offense. When Jacob returns to his homeland after cheating his brother, we expect hatred and vengeance from Esau. Instead, Esau welcomes Jacob with a joyful embrace, reversing Jacob's expectations no less than Jacob has already reversed Esau's fate. Similarly, King David treats his enemies with kindness and mercy, a policy that often seems shortsighted in its dismissal of traditional justice.

Another form of redemption involves the intervention of a third party as a mediator or sacrifice to quell God's anger with the wrongdoers. Moses's frantic prayers at Mount Sinai frequently cause God to "change his mind" and relent from destroying the Israelites (Exodus 32:14). In the Book of Judges, Samson sacrifices his life to redeem the Israelites from the Philistine oppression brought on by Israel's incessant evil. These human acts of redemption mirror God's promise in the religious laws to forgive the people's sins on the basis of ritual animal sacrifices and offerings.

THE VIRTUE OF FAITH

In the Old Testament, faith is a resilient belief in the one true God and an unshakable obedience to his will. The models of biblical faith are not those who are supported by organized religion but those who choose to trust in God at the most unpopular times. Part of the virtue of true faith is the ability to believe in God when he remains unseen. The Israelites betray their complete lack of faith when they complain after God repeatedly shows himself and displays miracles during the exodus from Egypt.

Noah, Abraham, and Elijah represent the three main heroes of faith in The Old Testament. Each demonstrates his faith in God by performing seemingly irrational tasks after God has been absent from humankind for an extended period of time. God has not spoken to humans for many generations when Noah obediently builds a large, strange boat in preparation for a monumental flood. Abraham similarly dismisses the idols and gods of his region in favor of a belief that an unseen and unnamed deity will provide a promised land for his descendants. Centuries later, the prophet Elijah attempts to rejuvenate faith in God after Israel has worshipped idols for decades. Like Noah and Abraham, Elijah develops a faith based on his ability to communicate directly with God.

MOTIFS

Motifs are recurring structures, contrasts, and literary devices that can help to develop and inform the text's major themes.

THE COVENANT

God's covenant with humankind incorporates both his promise

to grant Abraham and Abraham's descendants a promised land and the religious laws given to the Israelites. The covenant resembles ancient legal codes and treaties in which a lord or landowner specifies the conditions of a vassal's service and vows to protect the vassal in return. The biblical covenant, however, represents not just a contractual agreement but also a passionate, tumultuous relationship between God and humanity. God's covenant passes to Abraham's descendants, unifying the lives of seemingly disparate people within a developing story. The biblical writers suggest that this story is not theirs but God's—a means for God to show his purposes and his values to humankind by relating to one family.

The covenant is a unifying structure that allows the human characters to evaluate their lives as a series of symbolic experiences. At first, the signs of the covenant are physical and external. God relates to Abraham by commanding Abraham to perform the rite of circumcision and to kill his son, Isaac. In Exodus, God shows his commitment to the Israelites by miraculously separating the waters of the Red Sea and appearing in a pillar of fire. The religious laws are also symbols of the covenant. They represent customs and behavioral rules that unite the lives of the Israelites in a religious community devoted to God. Moses suggests that these laws are to become sacred words that the Israelites cherish in their hearts and minds (Deuteronomy 11:18). The covenant thus shapes the personal memories and the collective identity of the Israelites.

DOUBLES AND OPPOSITES

At the beginning of Genesis, God creates the world by dividing it into a system of doubles—the sun and the moon, light and dark, the land and the sea, and male and female. When

Adam and Eve eat the forbidden fruit, and when Cain kills his brother Abel, good and evil enter the world. From this point on, the Old Testament writers describe the world as a place of binary opposites, or sets of two basic opposing forces. These forces include positive and negative, good and bad, and lesser and greater. These distinctions characterize the ethics of the Israelites. The laws in Leviticus, Numbers, and Deuteronomy outline the criteria for being ceremonially clean or unclean, and for choosing obedience over disobedience.

Biblical writers frequently challenge these distinctions. As twins with opposing traits, Jacob and Esau represent ideal character doubles. When Jacob steals Esau's inheritance right, the younger son triumphs over the older son by dishonest, rather than honest, means. The reversal of fortune portrays God's covenant with humankind as a preference for the unexpected over the conventional, as well as God's willingness to accomplish his ends by imperfect means. The epic of Samson similarly blurs the line between weakness and strength. Samson, the icon of human strength, conquers the Philistines only after they bring him to his weakest by shaving his head and blinding him. Such stories question the human ability to tell the difference between good and bad.

GEOGRAPHY

The geography of the Old Testament determines the moral and religious well-being of the Hebrew people. The biblical authors circumscribe the spiritual story of Abraham and his descendants within a physical journey to and from the promised land. In a sense, the flow of the narrative can be summarized as a constant yearning for the promised land.

Displaced in Egypt, the Israelites grow in number without a religion or national identity. The journey with Moses to the promised land defines Israel's religion, laws, and customs. In Joshua, Judges, and the first book of Samuel, Israel's struggle to secure its borders mirrors its struggle to enjoy national unity and religious purity. David and Solomon's kingdoms represent the height of Israel, for Israel establishes a religious center in Jerusalem and begins to expand its territory. The division of the nation into northern and southern kingdoms represents the fragmentation of the promised land and, by implication, of God's promise to Israel. The ultimate exile into Assyria and Babylon denotes Israel's religious estrangement from God.

SYMBOLS

Symbols are objects, characters, figures, and colors used to represent abstract ideas or concepts.

THE FERTILE GROUND

The fertility of the earth symbolizes the quality of life of those who inhabit it. The garden paradise of Adam and Eve represents the ideal abundant existence for humanity. When God pronounces his curse to Adam, he curses the ground, vowing that humans will have to toil to produce food from the earth. God similarly destroys the ground when he sends the great flood. After Noah and his family emerge from the ark, however, the moist and fertile earth symbolizes the renewal of human life. When Joshua investigates the promised land in Numbers, he praises the region as a fruitful land that "flows with milk and honey" (Numbers 13:27). Biblical poetry frequently uses the image of fertile ground as a metaphor for human flourishing. In the Song of Solomon, a verdant, overgrown garden symbolizes the sexual maturity of a young woman. In Psalm 23, the psalmist emphasizes the herding culture of the ancient Hebrew people, characterizing God's peace as a shepherd who guides a sheep to green pastures.

THE ARK OF THE COVENANT

The Ark of the Covenant is Israel's chief symbol of God. The Israelites fashion the golden vessel at Mount Sinai according to God's instructions. The Ark contains a copy of the religious laws as well as a container of the heavenly food, manna. God's spirit or presence is said to reside between the two angels on the lid of the Ark in a space called "the mercy seat." The Ark's power is immense. When the Israelites carry it into the battle at Jericho, it ensures victory. When it is mistreated or dropped, or when it falls into the wrong hands, the Ark proves fatal to its handlers.

The Ark symbolizes the totality of all the symbols of God's covenant with the Israelites—it even represents God himself. As such, the Ark's location at each moment indicates Israel's commitment to the covenant. When the Ark does not have a permanent home or resting place, Israel's religious life remains disorganized. In the Book of Samuel, the Ark is actually stolen by the Philistines, representing a spiritual low-point for Israel. Israel's treatment of the Ark is thus emblematic of their reverence for God.

Summary and Analysis

Genesis: Chapters 1–11

Summary
The Book of Genesis opens the Hebrew Bible with the story of creation. God, a spirit hovering over an empty, watery void, creates the world by speaking into the darkness and calling into being light, sky, land, vegetation, and living creatures over the course of six days. Each day, he pauses to pronounce his works "good" (1:4). On the sixth day, God declares his intention to make a being in his "own image," and he creates humankind (1:26). He fashions a man out of dust and forms a woman out of the man's rib. God places the two people, Adam and Eve, in the idyllic garden of Eden, encouraging them to procreate and to enjoy the created world fully, and forbidding them to eat from the tree of the knowledge of good and evil.

In the garden, Eve encounters a crafty serpent who convinces her to eat the tree's forbidden fruit, assuring her that she will not suffer if she does so. Eve shares the fruit with Adam, and the two are immediately filled with shame and remorse. While walking in the garden, God discovers their disobedience. After cursing the serpent, he turns and curses the couple. Eve, he says, will be cursed to suffer painful childbirth and must submit to her husband's authority. Adam is cursed to toil and work the ground for food. The two are subsequently banished from Eden.

Sent out into the world, Adam and Eve give birth to two sons, Cain and Abel. Cain, a farmer, offers God a portion of his crops one day as a sacrifice, only to learn that God is more pleased when Abel, a herdsman, presents God with the fattest portion of his flocks. Enraged, Cain kills his brother. God exiles Cain from his home to wander in the land east of Eden. Adam and Eve give birth to a third son, Seth. Through Seth and Cain, the human race begins to grow.

Ten generations pass, and humankind becomes more evil. God begins to lament his creation and makes plans to destroy humankind completely. However, one man, Noah, has earned God's favor because of his blameless behavior. God speaks to Noah and promises to establish a special covenant with Noah and his family. He instructs Noah to build an ark, or boat, large enough to hold Noah's family and pairs of every kind of living animal while God sends a great flood to destroy the earth. Noah does so, his family and the animals enter the ark, and rain falls in a deluge for forty days, submerging the earth in water for more than a year. When the waters finally recede, God calls Noah's family out of the ark and reaffirms his covenant with Noah. Upon exiting the ark, Noah's family finds that the earth is moist and green again. God promises that from this new fertile earth will follow an equally fertile lineage for Noah and his family. But humankind must follow certain rules to maintain this favor: humans must not eat meat with blood still in it, and anyone who murders another human must also be killed. God vows never to destroy the earth again, and he designates the rainbow to be a symbol of his covenant.

One night, Noah becomes drunk and lies naked in his tent. Ham, one of Noah's sons, sees his naked father and tells his brothers, Shem and Japeth. Shem and Japeth cover their father without looking at him. Upon waking, Noah curses Ham's descendants, the Canaanites, for Ham's indiscretion, declaring that they will serve the future descendants of Ham's brothers. A detailed genealogy of the three brothers' descendants is given. Many generations pass and humankind again becomes corrupt. Some men, having moved west to Babylon, attempt to assert their greatness and power by building a large tower that would enable them to reach the heavens. Their arrogance angers God, who destroys the edifice. He scatters the people across the earth by confusing their common language, thus forever dividing humankind into separate nations.

ANALYSIS

The first eleven chapters of Genesis tell an authoritative story about the beginnings of the world that contains many contradictions. Scholars believe that the account is not the work of one author, but of a later editor or "redactor" who collected stories from various traditional sources into one volume. For instance, the author of the story of Cain and Abel shows a knowledge of Jewish sacrificial law that only a later writer would possess. Also, the narrator's introduction of stories with phrases such as "This is the list of the descendants of Adam" (5:1) or "These are the descendants of Noah" (6:9) suggests these tales existed before the current writer or redactor collected them into their present form.

The major thematic link of the first eleven chapters is the structuring of the world around a system of parallels and contrasts. Light breaks into the darkness, land separates water, and "the greater light" of the sun opposes "the lesser light" of the moon (1:16). A more complex occurrence of parallel and contrast takes place with the account of man's creation. Man is not only made in the image of God, paralleling him, but woman, made from the man's rib, contrasts with man. The Genesis writer uses the poetic device of antistrophe, or the repetition of a line in reverse order, to highlight the parallels and contrasts in the creation of man:

> *So God created humankind in his image,*
> *in the image of God he created them;*
> *male and female he created them.*   1:27–29

The antistrophe suggests that the world is logically organized around binary opposites, or basic opposing forces. Positive and negative, work and rest, and day and night are among the many binary opposites that the first chapters of Genesis describe. Good and evil is probably the most consistently explored binary opposite in the Old Testament, and the story of Cain and Abel initiates a lengthy analysis of the difference between good and evil. Cain's deception and murder of Abel, as well as his evasive response to God's questioning, describe his evil as inherent in his character and unmitigated by other good traits. God's punishment, however, demonstrates both justice and mercy, establishing God as the absolute good that opposes Cain's absolute evil. God exiles Cain from God's presence, but marks Cain to protect him from the wrath of other people.

Images of the ground and of the earth recur in these chapters. In Genesis, mankind's relationship with the ground is often a measure of the quality and fullness of human life. God creates Adam from dust, and Adam's fate is connected to the earth when God curses him:

> *cursed is the ground because of you;*
> *in toil you shall eat of it. . . .*
> *you are dust,*
> *and to dust you shall return.*   3:17, 19

Cain is similarly cursed to the ground, for he is exiled from his home and sent to wander in a strange land. The ground is the object of God's rage when God sends the flood and, in some respects, when he destroys the Tower at Babel. However, the ground is also the symbol of God's blessing to Noah, for God's promise of fertility to Noah's family mirrors the green and plentiful quality of the earth.

In the account of Noah, God himself uses symbols as much as the authors of the story. God explicitly calls the rainbow a "sign," or symbol, of his covenant with humanity after the flood (9:12–13). God frequently uses physical objects to show his spiritual purposes. But unlike the Greek gods of Homer or other Near-Eastern deities, the Hebrew God is never depicted as limited or defined by these objects. Rather, the authors of Genesis suggest that God is telling an elaborate allegorical story through the act of creation and that as God manages the affairs of the earth, symbolic meaning is one of the primary ways in which he communicates with his creations.

The central purpose of these introductory chapters is to construct a detailed etiology, or explanation of the origins of the world. The author is trying to account for the way that certain unfavorable elements of everyday human life came into being. The etiological concerns are clear enough in these chapters. The writers and the redactors have collected stories that explain how evil and separate nations entered the world, why women must live in a society characterized by male standards, why we as humans must work to survive, and why our daily labor is always so hard.

GENESIS: CHAPTERS 12–25

> *I will make you exceedingly fruitful; and I will make nations of you, and kings shall come from you.*
> *(See* QUOTATIONS, *p. 106)*

SUMMARY

Nine generations of Shem's descendants, the Semites, pass. God calls on a man named Abram, living with his father Terah and his wife Sarai in Haran, a city in upper Mesopotamia. God makes a covenant with Abram, promising to make Abram's descendants into a great nation. Abram agrees to leave his home and move southwest to Canaan with his wife and his nephew, Lot, to a land that God has promised to give to Abram's descendants. Abram takes up residence there and erects a number of altars throughout the land as symbols of his devotion to God.

After a brief stay in Egypt, Abram becomes wealthy and returns to Canaan, where, with the help of only 318 men, he defeats a legion of marauding armies from the East that has descended upon Sodom, where Lot is currently living. The king of Sodom recognizes Abram for his great deed, and the priest Melchizedek blesses Abram with a gift of bread and wine. Abram returns home where God speaks to him again regarding his covenant. Abram's descendants, God promises, will be as numerous as the stars in the sky. A ceremony is performed in which God passes a blazing pot through pieces of sacrificed animals, symbolizing that his promise will not be broken. The writer notes that God considers Abram's faith in him as a form of righteousness.

Sarai cannot become pregnant, but she wants to give her husband an heir. To this end, she sends her handmaiden Hagar to sleep with Abram. When Sarai becomes upset because of Hagar's contempt, the handmaiden flees in fear. God speaks to Hagar and comforts her, promising her a son who will be a "wild ass of a man," and Hagar returns to give birth to Abram's first son, Ishmael (16:12). Once again, God speaks with Abram, this time enjoining Abram to remain blameless in his behavior and adding a new requirement to his everlasting covenant. Abram and all his descendants must now be circumcised as a symbol of the covenant, and God promises Abram a son through Sarai. The son is to be called Isaac, and it will be through Isaac that the covenant is fulfilled. God renames Abram "Abraham," meaning "father of many," and gives Sarai a new name, "Sarah."

One day, God appears to Abraham in the form of three men. The three men say that Sarah will have a son, but Sarah, who is now ninety years old, laughs. The three men travel toward the eastern cities of Sodom and Gomorrah to destroy the cities because of their flagrant wickedness and corruption. Abraham pleads on the cities' behalf, convincing the Lord not to destroy the cities if only a handful of good men can be found there. The men enter the city of Sodom, and Lot welcomes them into his home. Night falls, and the men of the city surround Lot's home, wishing to rape the three messengers. The messengers persuade Lot to flee the city with his family, telling him and his family not to look back as they leave. However, as God rains down burning sulfur on Sodom and Gomorrah, Lot's wife looks back at her home and is turned into a pillar of salt.

Abraham continues to gain political status in the area of Canaan, and Sarah eventually gives birth to Isaac. At Sarah's bidding, Abraham sends Hagar and Ishmael away. God again speaks to Abraham in a test, asking Abraham to kill his son, Isaac, as a sacrifice. Abraham quietly resolves to obey, and when he takes Isaac to the mountains, Isaac asks what animal they are going to sacrifice. Abraham replies that God will provide an offering. Isaac is laid on the altar, and just as Abraham is ready to strike, the angel of the Lord stops him. God is impressed with Abraham's great devotion and, once again, reaffirms his covenant.

Sarah dies. Abraham sends his chief servant to Abraham's relatives in Assyria to find a wife for Isaac, to prevent his lineage from being sullied by Canaanite influence. The servant prays to be guided to the correct wife for Isaac. God leads him to Rebekah, whom he brings back to Isaac. Isaac marries Rebekah, and Abraham dies soon thereafter.

ANALYSIS

This section contrasts with the earlier parts of Genesis by telling the extended story of one man, Abraham, and his family rather than combining stories, songs, and genealogies. Genesis traces Abraham's ancestry to Noah's son, Shem, in order to establish that Abraham is a member of both the Hebrew and Semitic peoples. Historically, tribes of nomadic people known as habiru—many of whom were Semitic—frequently moved among the ancient Canaanite cities; scholars believe that these nomads may be the roots of the Hebrew people. Whether or not Abraham was indeed the original ancestor of the Hebrew people is uncertain. But the story of Abraham is nevertheless significant to the religious tradition of faith and obedience it prescribes.

God's affirmation of his covenant with humankind now takes the form of an ongoing, personal relationship with a specific man and his descendants. The authors of Genesis describe God himself as a storyteller who uses the lives of the people who are obedient to him to describe a divine plot. God creates various symbols as reminders of the covenant, including the fiery pot at his second encounter with Abram, the custom of circumcision, and the renaming of Abram and Sarai. Poetic devices further emphasize the literary nature of the story and the importance of the covenant. God first verbalizes his covenant with Abram in the form of a song and later comforts Hagar in verse. These elements, especially the poetic, provide a break in the Genesis narrative, slowing down the plot and suggesting the grand, metaphysical significance of God's promise to Abraham.

These stories demonstrate the ways in which God gives dramatic rewards for absolute faith and obedience. At God's command, Abraham leaves his home to roam in a strange land; God's reward is to cause Abraham to discover great wealth.

Sarah, barren her entire life, gives birth to a son at the age of ninety, an event so unlikely that she laughs when she is told that it will occur. And finally, Abraham receives God's greatest praise when he obediently stands poised to kill the very son through whom God has promised to fulfill his covenant. These moments depict absolute faith in God, despite the fact that his demands may seem illogical or unreasonable. What God consistently rewards is the abandonment of human reason and free will in favor of actions whose purpose is unknown or unknowable. As a result, these stories establish a version of God who knows what is best for mankind, but who reveals his purposes only selectively.

Another characteristic of the Old Testament God is the elusive manner in which he communicates with humans. Sometimes, people directly encounter God, as when God and Abraham converse. Frequently, however, God appears in the form of someone or something else, as when he visits Abraham in the form of three men. Throughout the Old Testament, God is alternately seen and unseen. Unlike the epics of the ancient Greeks, in which every event or action is described in full detail, there are always details in Genesis and the Hebrew Bible that remain unexplained because God so often insists on removing himself from the action. The most important instance of God's absence is when God tests Abraham. After requesting that Abraham sacrifice Isaac, God disappears without stating his true intentions, leaving Abraham to move forward in silence to the mountain where he will, supposedly, kill his son. In this story, God's absence serves the purpose of testing Abraham's faith in the infallibility of God, even when God does not explain his demands. Furthermore, the removal of God from the story greatly increases the drama and suspense of the Genesis narrative.

Genesis: Chapters 25–50

Summary

Following Abraham's death, God reveals to Isaac's wife Rebekah that she will soon give birth to two sons who will represent two nations, one stronger than the other. When Rebekah delivers, Esau is born first and is extremely hairy. Jacob, who is smooth skinned, is born immediately after, grasping the heel of his brother. Isaac's two sons grow to be opposites. Esau is a hunter and a brash man. Jacob stays at home, soft-spoken but quick-witted. One day, Esau comes home famished, demanding to be fed, and agrees to give Jacob his inheritance rights in exchange for a bowl of soup.

Like his own father, Isaac prospers in Canaan and, despite occasional errors in judgment, enlarges his property, making alliances with area rulers and continuing to erect monuments to God. One day, when he is old and blind, Isaac instructs Esau to catch some game and prepare him a meal so that he may give the elder son his blessing. While Esau is gone, Rebekah helps Jacob deceive his father, preparing a separate meal and disguising the younger son with hairy arms and Esau's clothing. When Jacob presents Isaac with the meal, Isaac—smelling Esau's clothing and feeling the hairy body—proceeds to bless Jacob, promising him the inheritance of God's covenant and a greater status than his brother. Esau returns to discover the deception, but it is too late. Isaac, though dismayed, says that he cannot revoke the stolen blessing.

Jacob flees in fear of Esau, traveling to the house of his uncle Laban in upper Mesopotamia. En route, Jacob dreams of a stairway leading up to heaven, where angels and God reside. In the dream, God promises Jacob the same covenant he previously made with Abraham and Isaac. Jacob arrives at Laban's house, where he agrees to work for his uncle in exchange for the hand of Laban's daughter, Rachel, in marriage. Laban deceives Jacob into marrying Leah, Rachel's older sister, before marrying Rachel. The two wives compete for Jacob's favor and, along with their maids, give birth to eleven sons and a daughter.

After twenty years, Jacob heeds God's urging and leaves to return to Canaan, taking his family, his flocks, and Laban's collection of idols, or miniature representations of gods. Rachel, who has stolen the idolic figurines from her father, hides them under her skirt when Laban tracks down the fleeing clan in the desert. Unable to procure his belongings, Laban settles his differences with Jacob, who erects a pillar of stone as a "witness" to God of their peaceful resolution (31:48). Jacob continues on and, nearing home, fears an encounter with Esau. Jacob prepares gifts to appease his brother and, dividing his family and belongings into two camps, spends the night alone on the river Jabbok. Jacob meets God, who, disguised as a man, physically wrestles with Jacob until dawn. Jacob demands a blessing from his opponent, and the man blesses Jacob by renaming him "Israel," meaning, "he struggles with God."

The next morning, Jacob meets Esau, who welcomes his brother with open arms. Jacob resettles in Shechem, not far from Esau, who has intermarried with the Canaanites and produced a tribe called the Edomites. Jacob and his sons prosper in peace until one day Jacob's daughter, Dinah, is raped by a man from Shechem. Enraged, Jacob's sons say they will let the Shechemite marry Dinah if all the members of the man's family will be circumcised. The man agrees and, while the greater part of his village is healing from the surgical procedure, Jacob's sons take revenge and attack the Shechemites, killing all the men. Isaac and Rachel die soon thereafter.

Jacob's sons grow jealous of their youngest brother, Joseph, who is Jacob's favorite son. When Jacob presents Joseph with a beautiful, multi-colored coat, the eleven elder brothers sell Joseph into slavery, telling their father that Joseph is dead. Joseph is sold to Potiphar, a high-ranking official in Egypt, who favors the boy greatly until, one day, Potiphar's flirtatious wife accuses Joseph of trying to sleep with her. Potiphar throws Joseph in prison, but—ever faithful to God—Joseph earns a reputation as an interpreter of dreams. Years pass until the Pharaoh of Egypt, bothered by two troublesome dreams, hears of Joseph and his abilities. Pharaoh summons Joseph, who successfully interprets the dreams, warning Pharaoh that a great famine will strike Egypt after seven years. Impressed, Pharaoh elects Joseph to be his highest official, and Joseph leads a campaign throughout Egypt to set aside food in preparation for the famine.

Famine eventually plagues the land and, learning of the Egyptian supply of grain, Joseph's brothers go to Egypt to purchase food. The eleven men present themselves to Joseph, who recognizes them immediately but refrains from revealing his identity. Joseph toys with his brothers to test their good will, first throwing them in jail and then sending them back to Canaan to retrieve their newest brother, Benjamin. They return with the boy, and Joseph continues his game, planting a silver cup in the boy's satchel and threatening to kill the boy when the cup is discovered. When Judah offers his own life in exchange for Benjamin's, Joseph reveals his identity. Joseph persuades his brothers to return to Egypt with Jacob, who, overjoyed, moves to Egypt with his family of seventy.

As Jacob approaches death, he promises Joseph that the covenant will pass on through Joseph and his two sons, Manasseh and Ephraim. However, when Jacob places his hands on the two boys to bless them, he crosses his arms, placing his right hand on

Ephraim, the younger son. Joseph protests, but Jacob says that Ephraim will be greater than Manasseh. Jacob dies soon thereafter and, accompanied by Egyptians, Joseph buries his father in Canaan. They return to Egypt, where Jacob's descendants, the Israelite people, grow rapidly. Joseph eventually dies, instructing his family to return one day to the land God has promised to give to Abraham, Isaac, and Jacob.

ANALYSIS

The division of the world into binary opposites, initiated with the creation story, dominates the latter half of Genesis. Just as light absolutely opposes darkness and male absolutely opposes female in the creation story, Esau and Jacob are diametrically opposed in everything from their appearance to their occupations and behavior. Rachel and Leah constitute another pair of binary opposites, struggling with each other for Jacob's affections. Oppositions continue, not only between Joseph's sons, Ephraim and Mannasseh, but with other, more intangible elements, such as the wrestling match between God and man, the contrast between abundance and famine in Egypt, and the decidedly joyful welcome of Esau after Jacob's expectations of a violent homecoming. Alongside the motif of opposites runs a motif of substitution or crossing; Jacob is blessed instead of Esau, and Jacob himself crosses his arms when he blesses Joseph's sons, bestowing the higher blessing on the younger son.

These opposing elements generate both irony and radical reversals in the stories of Isaac, Jacob, and Joseph. Esau does not merely receive a lesser blessing because Jacob steals his inheritance but is actually cursed to serve his younger brother forever, barred from the covenant entirely. Characters are increasingly tricky or deceptive in these stories, and their skill at deception usually earns them praise and privilege rather than punishment. Jacob deceives Esau, and as a result becomes the founder of one of the greatest nations in the Old Testament. Laban deceives Jacob, and receives twice as many years of service from him as a result. Rachel hides her father's idols under her dress, and Jacob's sons murderously trick the Shechemites. The most interesting deception, on a literary level, is Joseph's decision to veil his identity from his brothers. The elaborate deception builds in suspense over four chapters, as the narrative does not make it clear whether Joseph plans to enact revenge or simply to scare his brothers. When Judah offers to give his life for Benjamin, and Joseph forgives his brothers, trickery is replaced by the possibility of redemption, foreshadowing God's plan to reverse the Israelites' fortune with a promise of abundance in a new land.

Joseph plays a game of punishment and redemption with his brothers, and God plays the same game with the whole of humanity throughout Genesis. God creates a realm of opposing forces, symbols, and reversals to suggest a pattern of how and through whom his covenant will be revealed. The game is in the foreground, while God and his reasons for playing the game move into the background of the Genesis narrative. The game becomes literal rather than figurative when God wrestles Jacob by the Jabbok River. The event is a metaphor for how God conveys his promise to humankind in the second half of Genesis. Just as the mysterious man never identifies himself to Jacob, so God recedes further and further from humankind. Jacob, however, is able to see past his opponent's bodily appearance because he is persistent and faithful, eventually able to wrest a blessing from this obscured manifestation of God. The giving of the name "Israel" to Jacob not only commemorates this specific struggle but also commemorates the struggle of the Israelites with an unseen God. Joseph, the ancestor of the Israelites, never has an explicit conversation with God, yet he notes in the final chapter of Genesis that the happy outcome of the first trick his brothers play on him has helped to save many lives in Egypt. The experience of Joseph and Jacob shows that God's covenant is fulfilled largely through the act of struggling.

EXODUS

SUMMARY

The Book of Exodus begins more than four hundred years after Joseph, his brothers, and the Pharaoh he once served have all died. The new leadership in Egypt—feeling threatened by Jacob's descendants, who have increased greatly in size—embarks on a campaign to subdue the Israelites, forcing them into slavery and eventually decreeing that all Hebrew boys must be killed at birth in the Nile River. The Hebrew women resist the decree, and one woman opts to save her newborn son by setting him afloat on the river in a papyrus basket. Fortunately, Pharaoh's daughter discovers the abandoned child and raises him after he has been nursed, naming him Moses.

Moses is aware of his Hebrew roots, and, one day, he kills an Egyptian who is beating an Israelite worker. Moses flees in fear to Midian, a town near Sinai, where he meets a priest named Jethro and marries the man's daughter, beginning a new life as a shepherd. God, however, is concerned for the suffering of the Israelites, and he appears to Moses in the form of a burning bush. God speaks to Moses, informing him of his plan to return the Israelites to Canaan—to "a land flowing with milk and honey" (3:8)—and to send Moses back to Egypt to accomplish this task. Moses is timid and resists, citing his lack of eloquence and abilities, and refuses to go. God is angered but encourages Moses, presenting him with a staff for performing miracles and instructing Moses to take his brother, Aaron, with him as an aid. When Moses asks God what his name is, God replies, "I AM WHO I AM" (3:14).

Moses and Aaron return to Egypt, where Moses organizes the Israelites and confronts the Pharaoh, demanding the release of the Hebrew people. Moses performs a miracle, turning his staff into a snake, but Pharaoh is unimpressed and only increases the workload for the Israelites. God responds by inflicting a series of ten plagues on Egypt. God turns the Nile River into blood, causes frogs to cover Egypt, turns all of the dust in Egypt to gnats, and causes swarms of flies to come into the houses of Pharaoh and his officials. God then strikes Egypt's livestock with a disease, creates festering boils on humans and animals, and sends thunder, hail, and fire that destroy crops, livestock, and people. God sends swarms of locusts, and covers Egypt with "a darkness that can be felt" (10:21). Before each plague, Moses demands the Israelites' release, and after each plague, God purposefully "hardens" Pharaoh so that he refuses the request (4:21, 7:22). The tenth and final plague kills all the firstborn males in Egypt. Before the plague, Moses instructs the Hebrew people to cover their door posts in the blood of a sacrificed lamb as a sign for God to protect their homes from his killings. Pharaoh relents and releases the more than 600,000 Israelites who, in turn, plunder the Egyptians' wealth. Upon leaving, Moses enjoins the Israelites to commemorate this day forever by dedicating their firstborn children to God and by celebrating the festival of Passover, named for God's protection from the final plague (12:14–43).

Guided by a pillar of cloud during the day and by fire during the night, Moses and the Israelites head west toward the sea. Pharaoh chases them. The Israelites complain that Moses has taken them to die in the wilderness, and Moses, at God's bidding, parts the sea for the people to cross. Pharaoh follows and Moses closes the waters back again, drowning the Egyptian army. Witnessing the miracle, the people decide to trust Moses, and they sing a song extolling God as a great but loving warrior. Their optimism is brief, and the people soon begin to worry about the shortage of food and water. God responds by sending the people food from heaven, providing a daily supply of quail and a sweet bread-like substance called manna. The people are required only to obey God's commandments to enjoy this food. Soon thereafter, the Israelites confront the warring Amalekite people, and God gives the Israelites the power to defeat them. During battle, whenever Moses raises his arms, the Israelites are able to rout their opponents.

Three months after the flight from Egypt, Moses and the Israelites arrive at Mount Sinai, where God appears before them, descending on the mountain in a cloud of thunder and lightning. Moses climbs the mountain, and God gives Moses two stone tablets with ten commandments inscribed on them regarding general, ethical behavior as well as an extended series of laws regarding worship, sacrifices, social justice, and personal property. God explains to Moses that if the people will obey these regulations, he will keep his covenant with Israel and will go with them to retrieve from the Canaanites the land promised to Abraham. Moses descends from the mountain and relates God's commandments to the people. The people agree to obey, and Moses sprinkles the people with blood as a sign of the covenant. Moses ascends to the mountain again where God gives him more instructions, this time specifying in great detail how to build a portable temple called an ark in which God's presence will dwell among the Israelites. God also emphasizes the importance of observing the Sabbath day of holy rest.

Moses comes down from the mountain after forty days, only to find that Aaron and the Israelites have now erected an idol—a golden calf that they are worshipping in revelry, in direct

defiance of the ten commandments. Moses breaks the stone
tablets on which God has inscribed the new laws, and God plans
to destroy the people. Moses intercedes on the Israelites' behalf,
begging God to relent and to remember his covenant. Pleased with
Moses, God is appeased and continues to meet with Moses face
to face, "as one speaks to a friend," in a special tent set aside for
worship (33:11). God reaffirms his covenant with Moses, and,
fashioning new stone tablets to record his decrees, God declares
himself to be a compassionate, loving, and patient God. At
Moses's direction, the Israelites renew their commitment to the
covenant by erecting a tabernacle to God according to the exact
specifications God has outlined.

ANALYSIS

While Genesis explains the origins of the world and of humanity,
Exodus is the theological foundation of the Bible. Exodus explains
the origins of *Torah*—the law of the Jewish people and the tradition surrounding that law. Torah is not merely a list of laws, but,
rather, the notion of law as a way of life. Indeed, the law exists
as a way of life for Moses and his people. Although portions of
Exodus are devoted to legal matters, the declaration of law in
Exodus always comes in the form of a story, relayed by discussions
between God and Moses, and between Moses and the people.

These laws and tradition are filled with symbols of God's
promise to the Israelites. In Genesis, God uses symbols such as the
rainbow and gives people new names, like Abraham, as signs of
his covenant. Such personalized signs are useful when communi-
cating a promise to a single person or family. In Exodus, however,
God attempts to communicate his promise to an entire nation of
people. Social laws about how the Israelites should treat their slaves
and annual festivals such as Passover are signs that a community of

people can easily recognize and share. In this sense, obedience to God's laws is less a means of achieving a level of goodness than it is a way for the people to denote their commitment to God's covenant.

The Hebrew word for "Exodus" originally means "names," and Exodus is often called the Book of Names. The book discusses the different names God takes and the various ways God manifests himself to the Israelites. When God tells Moses that his name is "I AM" (3:14), God defines himself as a verb (in Hebrew, *ahyh*) rather than a noun. This cryptic statement suggests that God is a being who is not subject to the limits of people's expectations or definitions. Most often, however, God reveals himself to the people through theophany: extraordinary natural phenomena that signal God's arrival or presence. Theophanic events in Exodus include the pillars of cloud and fire, the thunder at Mount Sinai, and the miraculous daily supply of manna. Such spectacles demonstrate God's attempts to prove his existence to a nation of doubting people from whom he has been decidedly absent for more than four hundred years. The unwillingness of the people to accept God's existence is never more apparent than when the Israelites worship a golden calf in the shadow of the thunderous Mount Sinai. As a result, God's final manifestation of himself is the tabernacle—specifically, the Ark of the Covenant, a golden vessel in which God's presence, or spirit, will reside. Like the law, the Ark is an effective symbol of God, for it is an object that the people not only build as a community according to God's specifications but also as a religious vessel that can be picked up and carried wherever Israel goes.

Moses is the first true hero we encounter in the Hebrew Bible. He manifests all the traits of a traditional hero. He overcomes timidity and inner strife. He challenges Pharaoh, leading Israel to great feats. And he wields his own weapon, the miraculous staff. These elements give Moses traditional heroic status, but Moses also presents us with a new type of hero—the religious priest. All of Moses's political and military dealings serve the one end of delivering the Israelites to God, physically moving them from Egypt to Mount Sinai and interceding to God for them when they disobey. As God declares early on, Moses is God's representative to the people, and Moses makes God's relationship with Israel a personal one. Instead of a series of incendiary explosions, Moses presents God's instructions to the people through conversation and conveys God's desire to destroy the Israelites by breaking the stone tablets in front of them. Most importantly, Moses's dialogue with God enables the author to portray God in softer, human terms—as someone who listens, grieves, and is actually capable of changing his mind.

LEVITICUS, NUMBERS, AND DEUTERONOMY

You shall love the Lord your God with all your heart,
and with all your soul, and with all your might.

(See QUOTATIONS, *p. 107*)

SUMMARY

Throughout Leviticus, Israel remains encamped at Mount Sinai while God appears in the Tent of Meeting, dictating to Moses his specifications regarding the Jewish ceremonial laws. The laws are extremely detailed, outlining every aspect of how and when religious offerings are to be presented to God. God gives the instructions himself, and his voice comprises the majority of the text. A brief narrative interlude describes the anointing of Aaron and his sons as Israel's priests. At the ceremony, God appears and engulfs the altar in a burst of flames, eliciting shouts of joy from the people. Soon after, God also sends fire to consume two of Aaron's sons when they neglect to make the right preparations for approaching the altar.

God lists various types of forbidden sexual behavior and discusses foods and physical conditions that can make a person unclean. Uncleanliness can result from things such as bodily discharge or touching a dead carcass. An unclean person must leave the Israelite camp or undergo physical cleansing, waiting periods, and religious sacrifices. Typically, sexual sins are punishable by death, but God also instructs the Israelites to kill a man who blasphemes, or curses God's name. Of all his restrictions, God places particular emphasis on the prohibition against eating meat with blood still in it: doing so will result in banishment, not only from Israel but from God's graces as well.

In the end, God promises to give Israel great abundance and success if it obeys these laws. If Israel is disobedient, though, God will send destruction and famine and "abhor" the Israelites (26:30). But the laws in Leviticus also set aside an annual Day of Atonement during which the priest is to offer sacrifices for the forgiveness of the entire nation. As long as the Israelites confess and repent for their sins, God promises to keep his covenant and never leave them.

At the beginning of Numbers, Israel prepares to continue the journey from Mount Sinai to the promised land. God devotes one of the twelve tribes, the Levites, to assist Aaron in the work of the priesthood, maintaining and watching over Israel's religious articles. After dedicating the Tabernacle, which houses the Ark of the Covenant, the Israelites leave Sinai, guided by the movements of a cloud that rests over the Tabernacle. Entering the desert, the people begin to complain about everything from the lack of interesting food to Moses's leadership.

Moses sends spies into Canaan to explore the promised land. Upon returning, two of the spies, Joshua and Caleb, report that

Israel can successfully conquer the Canaanite people with God's help. However, some of the spies incite an uprising, arguing that it will be impossible to take the land from the Canaanites and that Israel should return to Egypt instead. God plans to destroy the people for their lack of faith, but Moses intervenes and convinces God to forgive them. God relents but delivers a heavy curse. He announces that the current generation of Israelites, with the exception of Joshua and Caleb, will not be allowed to enter the promised land. Moses leads the people back toward the Red Sea to wander in the wilderness for a period of forty years.

Another revolt occurs when three men grow jealous of Moses's leadership. God plans to destroy the entire nation because of the men's jealousy, but Moses persuades God to destroy only the guilty parties. Moses warns the people that the men will die as a result of their own disobedience. God causes the ground to open and swallow the men, but the Israelites blame Moses and Aaron for the incident. Very angry, God sends a rapidly spreading plague through the crowd, killing thousands. Aaron runs out into the crowd and holds up the priest's censer to atone for Israel's wrongdoing, stopping the plague in its destructive path.

Following this event, Moses and Aaron themselves disobey God. The people continue to complain about the lack of water and express their longing to be back in Egypt. God instructs Moses to speak to a rock and command it to produce water. Moses, instead, hits the rock angrily with his staff. The rock proceeds to pour forth water, but God tells Moses and Aaron that they, too, will never enter the promised land because of this brash act. Aaron dies soon after, and the priesthood passes on to Aaron's son Eleazar.

Israel wanders in the lands southwest of Canaan, requesting safe passage from the surrounding nations but receiving little hospitality in return. With God's help, Israel conquers the Amorites and settles in their lands. Learning of the overthrow, the king of Moab summons a renowned sorcerer, Balaam, to come and pronounce a curse on the Israelites. The angel of God intercepts Balaam on the road to Moab, frightening Balaam's donkey. When Balaam strikes the panicked animal, the donkey miraculously speaks, rebuking Balaam. The Lord points out the angel's presence. The angel of God forbids Balaam to curse the Israelites before the king of Moab. Balaam arrives in Moab and delivers four cryptic oracles to the king, blessing Israel and predicting Moab's destruction.

The Israelite men succumb to the surrounding native peoples by fraternizing with the local women and worshipping the pagan god Baal. God sends a plague on Israel that ends only when Eleazar's son, the priest, kills an Israelite man and his Midianite mistress, stabbing them before all of Israel with a single thrust of his spear. Eleazar's son's impassioned act earns God's approval, and God leads Israel in destroying the Midianites, plundering their wealth in the process. As the forty-year waiting period draws to a close, God appoints Joshua to eventually succeed Moses as the people's leader.

The Book of Deuteronomy begins in the final, fortieth year of Israel's wandering in the desert. Stationed east of the Jordan River, Moses addresses the new generation of Israelites in preparation for entering the promised land. He summarizes the events of the past four decades and encourages the young Israelites to remember God's miracles and covenant with Israel. He forbids the worship of other gods or idols in the new land and repeats the Ten Commandments given by God at Mount Sinai. Most importantly, Moses gives explicit instructions to the Israelites to destroy all the native inhabitants of the promised land so that the Canaanites do not interfere with Israel's worship of God. Moses restates many of the social laws and rules of conduct outlined in Leviticus, adding a few new laws, such as the requirement for the Israelites to cancel debts every seven years.

Moses stresses God's love for Israel, describing God as someone who protects orphans, widows, and oppressed people. Israel is to love God intensely in return, with absolute devotion. The words of God's laws are very important. Moses instructs the Israelites to meditate on these words and to write the laws on their bodies and on the doorframes of their homes. Moses argues that the love of God and a commitment to his laws will be considered goodness for Israel (6:25). While Moses predicts that Israel will eventually grow disobedient, he notes that God will welcome Israel back with abundance and prosperity whenever Israel returns to obedience.

At God's direction, Moses composes a song that recounts Israel's history of unfaithfulness and extols God's everlasting compassion. Moses says the song will be a reminder to future Israelites of their covenant with God. He writes the song in the Book of the Laws and places the book with the Ark of the Covenant. Afterward, Moses ascends a mountain where God shows him a vision of the promised land. Moses dies and is buried by God. The author praises him as the only prophet in Israel's history who performed such impressive miracles and who knew God "face to face" (34:10).

ANALYSIS

The books of Leviticus, Numbers, and Deuteronomy form the bulk of the Hebrew law, or Torah. Each text mixes procedural instructions and legal matters with a variety of narrative voices and action. The separate books are probably the collected writings of priests with different interests and perspectives, written sometime during Israel's tumultuous exile in the seventh and sixth centuries B.C. The three works document an important stage in the development of Israel's identity as a people and a nation. The prose is frequently arduous and repetitive, but it functions as a long, concentrated pause in the narrative of the Old Testament. Israel's wandering in the desert can be seen as the nation's adolescence—a period of education and growth following the nation's birth in the exodus from Egypt and the events at Mount Sinai.

The fact that the Israelites' punishment for certain infractions is to isolate or expel the offending individual from the camp demonstrates the extraordinary desire of the people to remain part of the community. The Israelite camp is set up in concentric circles with the tabernacle at its center: Moses and Aaron are closest to the tabernacle, followed by the Levites who care for it, and the rest of the tribes surround them. Since uncleanness bars a person from approaching the sacred religious items, physical impurity places one farthest from the center of Israel. In this way, God's injunctions challenge the Israelites to strive to remain near the nation's center. The distinction between purity and impurity helps promote a distinction between an accepted, privileged "us" and an outcast "them" who are outside the circle of the community.

Moses's emphasis on the word "heart" in his sermons is also critical to Israel's understanding of itself as a unified people. Moses describes the physical and external regulations of the law by using spiritual and internal imagery. He says, "Hear, O Israel: The Lord is our God, the Lord alone. You shall love the Lord your God with all your heart, and with all your soul, and with all your might. Keep these words that I am commanding you today in your heart" (Deuteronomy 6:6). The idea that Israel as a whole has a "heart" or a group of "hearts" suggests that the nation has developed a set of personal or private experiences over the forty years of wandering in the desert. This waiting period distances Israel from Egypt and the laws at Mount Sinai, forcing the nation to form a collective memory of these events. When Moses instructs the people, "You shall put these words of mine in your heart and soul," he encourages them

to internalize and embrace these collective, national memories
(Deuteronomy 11:18). Moses portrays the religious laws no longer
as a list of actions to be performed in the future but as sacred words
and ideas that are a part of a past and an internal life that is unique
to Israel.

The description of God as loving and compassionate in
Deuteronomy is perplexing in light of God's intense wrath in
Numbers. Moses, however, seems to see God's violent reaction to
Israel's complaints and infidelities as an exercise or a test of Israel's
commitment to the covenant. Indeed, God's destruction follows
a consistent pattern in Numbers: the people complain and wish
to return to Egypt; God threatens to destroy the people; Moses
or another representative intercedes on behalf of the people; and
God relents, punishing only a portion of Israel's population. The
climax in these exercises occurs when representatives of the people
speak on behalf of Israel. The moment of intercession when the
plague is stopped by Aaron running into the crowd or by Eleazar's
son stabbing the man and his foreign mistress are both climactic.
Man's intercession does not require God to stop his destruction,
but it creates the opportunity for Israel's leaders to display religious
zeal and for God to show his mercy. God manifests his compassion
and love not by what he does, but by what he does not do. Israel
emerges from these encounters as a nation that has survived trials
and hardship—a resilient people, with its weakest members now
weeded out.

JOSHUA

SUMMARY
After the death of Moses, God calls on Joshua to lead the Israelites
across the Jordan River and take possession of the promised land.

God guarantees victory in the military campaign and vows never to leave the Israelites so long as they obey his laws. The people swear their allegiance to Joshua, and he sends two spies across the river to investigate the territory. The men enter Jericho, where a prostitute named Rahab hides them in her home and lies to the city officials regarding the spies' presence. Rahab tells the spies that the Canaanites are afraid of Israel and its miraculous successes. Professing belief in the God of the Israelites, she asks for protection for her family when the Israelites destroy Jericho. The spies pledge to preserve Rahab and return to Joshua, telling him of the weakened condition of Israel's enemies.

The Israelites cross the Jordan River, led by a team of priests carrying the Ark of the Covenant. As the priests enter the water, the flow of the river stops and the Israelites cross the river on dry land. Arriving on the other side, the Israelites commemorate the miracle with an altar of twelve stones from the river bed (representing the twelve tribes of Israel). The people begin to eat the produce of the new land—thus halting the daily supply of manna—and the Israelite men perform the ritual of circumcision in preparation for battle.

Approaching Jericho, Joshua encounters a mysterious man who explains that he is the commander of God's army but that he is neither for nor against Israel. Joshua pays homage to the man and passes on. Following divine instructions, Joshua leads the Israelites in carrying the Ark around Jericho for six days. On the seventh day, the Israelites march around the city seven times. Joshua rallies them to conquer the city and kill everyone except for Rahab. They are to refrain from taking any of the city's religious items. At the sound of the Israelite war cry, the walls of Jericho collapse, and the Israelites destroy the city and its inhabitants.

Joshua's fame spreads throughout the land, but the Israelites are humiliated in their attempts to take the next city, Ai. God attributes the disaster to the disobedience of Achan, an Israelite who has stolen religious items from Jericho. After the people stone Achan, the renewed attempt against Ai is successful as Joshua masterminds an elaborate ambush against the city's forces. The Israelites celebrate by erecting an altar to God and publicly reaffirming their commitment to God's law.

Fearful of the marauding Israelites, the people of Gibeon visit the Israelite camp in disguise, claiming to be travelers in the land and requesting peace with Israel. Joshua does not inquire with God and makes a hasty treaty with the men, only to discover later that the Gibeonites are natives of the land to be conquered. The Israelites refrain from attacking the city, but five other local kings attack Gibeon for making peace with Israel. The Israelites come to Gibeon's aid and destroy the five armies. Joshua helps by commanding God to make the sun stand still during the fight. God listens and stops the sun's movement—the only time in history, we are told, when God obeys a human.

The Israelites continue to destroy the southern and northern cities of Canaan, killing all living inhabitants, as God has stipulated. While much of the promised land still remains to be conquered, the people of Israel begin to settle in the land, dividing it amongst the twelve tribes. After God gives Israel rest from its enemies for many years, an ailing Joshua makes a farewell pronouncement to the nation of Israel. Joshua goads the Israelites to be strong and to obey all of God's laws, throwing away any idols and refraining from intermarriage with the native people. The people assure Joshua they will be faithful to the covenant, but Joshua reluctantly accepts this assurance, worried that obedience for Israel will prove quite difficult.

ANALYSIS

Scholars dispute the historical accuracy of the Book of Joshua. Although the writer claims to be writing in the thirteenth century B.C., it is unlikely that Joshua was written that early, and it is unlikely that the conquest of Palestine by the Hebrew people was as clean and neat as the first twelve chapters of Joshua suggest. Some scholars choose to read the book not as an inaccurate record of history but as an accurate record of Hebrew cultural memory of the original invasion of Palestine by the wandering Israelites. Unlike Genesis and Exodus, Joshua contains detailed accounts of political and military battles, and more than half of the book is devoted to listing the allotment of land to each of the twelve tribes. Few of the characters are as dramatic as those in the first books of the Old Testament, and God interferes little with human lives. In this sense, Joshua reads more like an ancient Hebrew history textbook than a collection of separate myths and legends.

The Book of Joshua carefully structures its description of the invasion of Palestine. The strict organization of the book emphasizes that the description of the conquests is a literary interpretation, and shows the importance within this interpretation of the idea of land. Israel's conquest is divided into two parts: the first twelve chapters tell the story of the conquest itself, and the final twelve chapters tell the story of how the land was allotted. These two sections are each subdivided into two sections. In these four parts, Israel prepares for the conquest, the campaigns themselves are carried out, the conquered land is allotted, and a concluding section exhorts Israel to remain loyal to God. The geographic organization of the book is equally rigorous; both the conquests and the division of lands are grouped according to whether the lands are in the north, south, east, or west. In the process, the idea of land plays a role as antagonistic as any character's. Various people's desire for and loyalty to specific regions is a source of great conflict, and God's covenant with Israel is physically manifested in his promise of land.

The Book of Joshua describes Joshua as an echo of Moses who engages in the same actions, only of lesser magnitude and with lesser effect. Moses leads the Israelites out of their oppression in Egypt; Joshua leads them into their domination of Canaan. Furthermore, Joshua causes the Jordan River to run dry in the same way that Moses parts the Red Sea. Finally, both Joshua and Moses perform similar administrative actions, sending out spies and allotting land to tribes. However, the differences between Moses's and Joshua's stories almost always indicate that Moses was a grander leader and prophet. While Moses communes directly with God, speaking with him face to face as though to a friend, God's presence in the Book of Joshua is largely symbolic. God exists for them in the Ark of the Covenant, a container that contains the text of Mosaic law. He does not, however, take physical form. Moses both foreshadows and overshadows Joshua.

This simplified rendering of the military campaign is contrasted by a lingering ambivalence in the behavior and the future of the Israelite people throughout Joshua. Rahab may display a blind faith in God, and the treaty with the Gibeonites may be the result of a deception, but by sparing these figures the Israelites disobey God's ongoing commandment to destroy all the native inhabitants of the promised land. Equally perplexing is the man or angel who is "the commander of the army of the Lord." He claims to be neither for nor against Israel, yet his presence at the battle of Jericho seems to connote God's blessing on Israel's military exercises. The ten chapters describing the allotment of tribal lands also undercut the decisive victories depicted in the first half of the book. Israel's resettlement is a project of enormous proportions, occurring before all the land has even been conquered. In fact, it is not clear if the remaining lands will ever be conquered; but, although God requires the total conquest of the promised land, he nevertheless gives them rest from battle (23:1). Finally, in his farewell to Israel, Joshua commands the people to throw away their religious idols and to refrain from allying with the native people. At no point do the people agree to either stipulation. Instead, they merely affirm that they will serve God (24:18, 24). Paradoxically, Joshua responds, "You cannot serve the Lord, for he is a holy God" (24:19). The ambivalence of the people regarding obedience to God in light of Joshua's persistence suggests that the future of Israel is uncertain at best.

JUDGES

SUMMARY

After Joshua's death, the tribes of Israel continue their conquest of the southern regions of Canaan, but they are unable to cleanse the land thoroughly of its native inhabitants. God declares that these remaining people will be an impediment to Israel's enjoyment of the promised land. Generations pass, and the younger Israelites turn away from God, intermarrying with the Canaanites and worshipping the local deities. God threatens to abandon Israel because of the disobedience of the youth, but he selects a series of judges, or rulers, to act as temporary leaders for the people.

Throughout the lives of these judges, the narrator tells us, Israel's behavior follows a consistent pattern: the people of Israel fall into evil, God sends a leader to save them, and, once the judge dies, the people commit even greater evil. When the Israelites' continued worship of the Canaanite gods leads to an invasion by the nation of Moab, God sends Israel a left-handed man named Ehud to be its deliverer. Ehud visits the Moabite king and offers to give the king a secret message from God. When the king dismisses his attendants, Ehud draws a sword strapped to his right thigh and plunges it into the obese king, killing him. Ehud escapes and leads the Israelites in regaining control of the Jordan River valley.

A prophet named Deborah emerges as Israel's new judge after Israel returns to evil and is invaded by a mighty army from the north. Counseling Israel's tribes under a great tree, she calls for an insurrection, and, together with God's help, the Israelites defeat the king's 900 chariots, sending the Canaanite general, Sisera, into retreat. When Sisera seeks refuge in a local woman's tent, the owner, Jael, lures Sisera to sleep and kills him, hammering a peg into his skull. Deborah recounts the victory in a lengthy song, extolling God as a warrior and herself as the "mother in Israel" (5:7).

God commissions a humble man, Gideon, to save Israel from its next invaders, the Midianites, who impoverish and scatter the people. Gideon tears down his father's altar to the god Baal, and the Israelites respond in droves to his call to fight. God demands fewer men for the battle, and, in a test, Gideon leads the men to a river to drink. Those who cup their hands to drink are sent home, and the remaining three hundred men who lap the water with their tongues are chosen for God's army. Spying on the enemy troops at night, Gideon overhears a Midianite soldier tell his friend about a dream in which a small loaf of bread was able to knock down a large Midianite tent. The friend interprets the dream as a sign that Midian will be defeated by Israel. Gideon and his few men surround the camps, and—with the sound of trumpets and broken jars—the Israelites emit such a clamorous war cry that the Midianites turn and slay each other. Israel attempts to make Gideon its king, but Gideon refuses, proclaiming that God alone is ruler of Israel.

Widespread worship of the god Baal plagues Israel, and Gideon's son Abimelech serves a violent three-year reign as Israel's king. His tyrannical reign ends when a woman throws a millstone on Abimelech's head. Pressured by the Philistines from the east and the Ammonites from the west, Israel turns from its idol worship and God selects a new judge, Jephthah, the son of a prostitute, to challenge the Ammonites. Jephthah promises God that, if he is victorious, he will sacrifice to God the first thing that comes out of his house the day he returns from battle. Upon devastating the Ammonites, Jephthah returns home to see his daughter emerge from his house, dancing, to greet him. Jephthah laments his promise, but his daughter encourages him to remain faithful to God, and Jephthah kills the virgin girl.

The Philistines continue to oppress Israel, and the angel of God appears to a childless Israelite couple, promising them a son who will become Israel's next deliverer. The couple raises their son, Samson, as a Nazirite—a person who symbolizes his devotion to God by never cutting his hair. God blesses Samson with exceptional abilities, and one day Samson kills a lion with his bare hands. Contrary to his parents' urging, Samson chooses a Philistine woman to be his wife. During the wedding ceremony, he baffles the Philistines with a riddle, the answer to which they discover only when Samson's wife reveals the answer to them. Samson burns with anger and goes home without his wife, but when he returns to retrieve her, the Philistines have given her to another man. Samson captures three hundred foxes and ties torches to each of their tails, setting the Philistine crops ablaze. When the Philistines pursue Samson, the Israelites hand him over to his enemies, bound at the wrist. With God's power, Samson breaks his bindings and uses the jaw-bone of a donkey to kill a thousand Philistine men.

Again, Samson falls in love with a Philistine woman, Delilah. The Philistine officials urge Delilah to discover the secret of Samson's strength. Three times, Delilah asks Samson the source of his power, and Samson lies to her each time, duping the officials in their attempts to subdue him. After a while, Samson tells her the truth, informing her that his long hair is the source of his strength. While Samson is asleep, Delilah has his hair cut and alerts the officials, who capture him and gouge out his eyes. In prison, Samson's hair begins to grow again, and, during a Philistine religious festival, the blind Samson is brought out to entertain the crowds. Samson asks his servant to guide him to the pillars of the arena, and—crying out to God—Samson knocks down the pillars of the temple, killing the Philistine rulers.

Without a judge, Israel becomes even more corrupt. One day, a man and his concubine are accosted while spending the night in the Israelite tribe of Benjamin. When a gang of Benjamite men demand to have sex with the man, he offers them his concubine instead, and the men rape her repeatedly throughout the night until she dies. Enraged, the man brings the concubine home and cuts her into twelve pieces, sending a piece to each of the twelve tribes of Israel as a symbol of Israel's corruption. The rest of Israel rallies together in opposition to the tribe of Benjamin, and, with God's help, the united tribes kill more than 25,000 Benjamites. Israel grieves for its lost tribe and helps the remaining Benjamites repopulate their land.

ANALYSIS

Biblical scholars typically group the books of Joshua and Judges together, noting how well the two works complement each other. On the one hand, Joshua purports to tell a chronological history of the Hebrew conquest of Canaan, but the account and the conquest itself seem too perfect to be accurate. In contrast, Judges is a compilation of myths about the early years of the Israelite settlement. While the stories are indeed fanciful, they suggest a gradual and disjointed occupation of the promised land that is probably more true to history than the Book of Joshua. While Joshua provides a methodical description of the various battles and an explanation of the distribution of land, Judges reveals the stories that the Israelite conquerors told as they gradually took over.

These individual accounts of Israel's judges are myths in the true sense of the word—not because they are false but because they are important to early Hebrew culture. The central theme of these myths is heroic struggle, chiefly of marginalized or oppressed people. The Israelites in the Book of Judges are strangers in a land they have recently conquered, and they are pressured from all sides by powerful regimes. Israel's judges manifest the virtues of this marginalized status. Jephthah is the son of a prostitute. The narrator takes pains to note that Ehud is left-handed, and it is this characteristic that enables Ehud to draw his sword and kill the Moabite king by surprise. Even more important than Deborah as a female hero is Jael, who uses the pretense of feminine warmth to draw a great commander into her tent, comforting him before she kills him.

The myth of Samson may be more appropriately described as an epic, because it is a relatively long story concerning the development of a single, extraordinary hero who, it might be said, is a metaphor for ancient Israel itself. Samson epitomizes some interesting dualities—brute nature versus civilized culture, strength versus weakness, Hebrew versus Philistine. What is unique to this story and to Judges as a whole, is that, unlike earlier books, the struggle between these opposing forces does not serve to develop irony or reversal. For Samson, the line between these distinctions is blurred. Samson—defined more by his identity as a Nazirite—is a displaced man, roaming back and forth between his home and Philistine, falling in love with Philistine women yet terrorizing the Philistines, and eventually suffering betrayal by the Israelites in return. It is only when Samson destroys the temple, crying out, "Let me die with the Philistines!" that Israel is saved through Samson's service (16:30). The epic of Samson shows that Israel's struggle—and its salvation—consists less of cleansing foreign influences from the land than of grappling with those influences while remaining faithful to God.

The stories in Judges are filled with extreme violence. This violence may cause us to question how God can be good if the greater part of the tribe of Benjamin is killed to make a religious point, or if Jephthah must keep his promise to God by killing his daughter. One answer is that the abundant violence in Israel is not due to God's wrath but to Israel's wickedness. Israel promiscuously worships other gods and insists on returning to evil despite God's help. Another, more subtle answer is that death in Judges is not always an absolute evil but is, at times, a thing of beauty. The tales in Judges begin to develop the notion of sacrifice—the idea that one person's death can be meaningful to another person, for religious or ethical reasons. Samson's death saves Israel from Philistine persecution, and Sisera's death at Jael's hands is a poignant symbol of Israel's victory to be celebrated in song (5:24–30). The writer tells us that the sacrifice of Jephthah's virgin daughter becomes a tradition among the Israelites, an annual celebration of the story by adolescent girls to symbolize passage from innocence into womanhood (11:39–40).

The First Book of Samuel

Because you have rejected the word of the Lord,
he has also rejected you from being king.
                    (See QUOTATIONS, *p. 108)*

SUMMARY

Israel's next judge, Samuel, is born to Hannah, a previously barren woman. Hannah gives Samuel to Israel's chief priest, Eli, to be raised as a Nazirite. The priesthood in Israel is in a general state of decline, and Eli's sons are disobeying God's laws. God declares that he will choose a new priest for Israel from outside Eli's family and begins delivering messages to Samuel as a young man. Samuel becomes a recognized prophet throughout Israel, delivering God's messages to the people.

During battle, the Philistines kill Eli's sons and capture the Ark of the Covenant—Israel's religious altar and symbol of God. Upon learning of the attack and robbery, Eli falls over and dies. The Ark is returned to Israel after it causes its Philistine captors to become terribly diseased. As the nation rejoices, Samuel persuades Israel to set aside its worship of local pagan deities, and God helps Israel thwart Philistine oppression for many years.

The Israelites demand that Samuel appoint a king for them so that Israel will be like other nations. Samuel is displeased, but God grants him permission to elect a king. God notes that by asking for a king, the people have not rejected Samuel; they have rejected God. Samuel warns the people that a monarchy brings certain drawbacks such as taxation, the conscription of armed forces, and the potential for tyranny, but the people are resolute.

God tells Samuel who should be king, and the following day, a man named Saul appears before Samuel, inquiring about some lost donkeys. Samuel pours oil over Saul's head to anoint him as king, and God provides a series of mystical signs to assure Saul that he should be king. Saul, who is a head taller than the average man, pleases the Israelites as king and leads them in rescuing an Israelite outpost from invasion. Stepping down as Israel's leader, Samuel encourages the people that, so long as they are obedient to God's laws, God will not punish them for requesting a king.

Despite many military victories, Saul soon disobeys God. He tries to rush into battle by performing a ritual war sacrifice without the help of a priest. Later, Samuel sends Saul to fight the Amalekites, instructing Saul to destroy them completely and leave nothing alive. Saul, however, spares the Amalekite ruler and the best portion of their flocks, hoping to present them as sacrifices to God. Samuel rebukes Saul, claiming that obedience to God's instructions is more important than religious sacrifice. He informs Saul that God will choose another man to be king of Israel. Saul pleads with Samuel, begging for forgiveness. Saul grabs for Samuel's cloak, but the cloth tears—a symbol, says Samuel, of Saul's broken kingdom.

God leads Samuel to the town of Bethlehem to choose a new king from Jesse's family. Each of Jesse's older sons are impressive, but God instructs Samuel to judge people not by their external appearances but, rather, by their hearts. Samuel anoints Jesse's youngest son, David, a shepherd, as king, and God gives divine power to David. God withdraws his power from Saul, cursing Saul with psychological distress in the form of an "evil spirit" (16:14). David begins his rise to courtly status as a harp-player for Saul during the king's emotional unrest.

The Philistines again threaten to attack Israel, this time taunting Israel with their new hero, Goliath—a giant more than nine feet tall. Saul and the Israelites tremble in fear, but David, arriving to deliver food to his brothers, offers to fight the giant. Refusing the king's armor, David publicly invokes God's help and kills Goliath with a single stone shot from his sling. The Israelites attack the retreating Philistines, and Israel returns home to the sound of women singing praises of David's victory.

Saul is insanely jealous of David, who becomes an intimate friend of Saul's son, Jonathan, and leads the Israelite troops to many more victories. After attempting to kill David with a spear, Saul sends David on a suicide mission to kill a hundred Philistine men and bring back their circumcised foreskins. David succeeds, and Saul grudgingly rewards David with his daughter Michal's hand in marriage. Saul orders his household to kill David, but, with the help of Michal and Jonathan, David flees from Saul. David builds an army of unhappy and impoverished Israelites, and he is joined by a priest who is also fleeing from Saul's destructive path.

Saul pursues David into the desert where David spares the king's life twice. While Saul is urinating in a cave, David sneaks up behind him and cuts off a corner of Saul's robe, scorning the opportunity to kill God's "annointed" ruler (24:6). At night, David and his men sneak into the king's tent and steal Saul's spear while he is sleeping. On both occasions, David announces his deed to Saul, and Saul expresses remorse both times, begging for David's mercy.

Still, Saul continues his pursuit, and David takes refuge with the Philistines, who show mercy to the great warrior and adversary of Israel's king. Preparing to fight the Philistines, Saul is wracked with fear and consults a witch, bidding the spirit medium to conjure up the dead spirit of Samuel. Samuel's ghost angrily warns Saul that he and his sons will die fighting the Philistines, ensuring the demise of Saul's kingdom. David and his men head out to fight the Amalekites, and David succeeds in destroying the warring nation. In the meantime, Saul leads Israel into a losing battle with the Philistines, and Saul's sons, including Jonathan, are killed. Saul commands his armor-bearer to kill him, but the boy refuses, and Saul falls on his own sword and dies.

ANALYSIS

The first book of Samuel tells the story of Israel's transition from a theocracy, or state ruled by a religious leader, to a monarchy, or state ruled by a political leader. Israel starts out as a nation of loosely affiliated tribes led by priests and religious heroes, but it becomes a nation-state led by a centralized king. Each stage of this transition is depicted through the narrative's three main figures: Samuel represents the old rule of the judges, Saul represents Israel's failed attempt at monarchy, and David represents God's ideal king. Although it seems logical that the rule of a single king would bring a sense of unity and cohesiveness to Israel, the opposite is the case. The move away from religious leaders divides religious and political life in Israel. Confusion about how religion and politics ought to relate to one another is the chief source of conflict in Samuel. Indeed, Saul's gravest mistake as king is his attempt to carry out the sacrificial duties of the priesthood—a role that Samuel explicitly denies the political ruler.

God's ambivalence regarding the monarchy escalates this conflict. On the one hand, God and Samuel are displeased at Israel's demand for a king, because, as God claims, this demand represents Israel's refusal to believe that God and his religious laws are adequate to rule the people. On the other hand, God willingly chooses Saul to be king, identifying Saul as the deliverer of his people. God reconciles this contradiction by distinguishing Israel's status as a human institution from its status as a divine one. As Samuel's warnings to Israel about the dangers of having a king suggest, God may bless the king, but he will not keep the king from committing the sorts of human errors and injustices that human rulers are prone to commit.

Saul's demise as king is tragic because he makes such small, human mistakes. Like all tragic heroes, Saul possesses a fatal flaw: he is more concerned with earthly objects and human customs than with spiritual or religious matters. Saul's plan to present the plunder from the Amalekites as a sacrifice to God earns Samuel's criticism because Saul mistakes a human custom for religious devotion. This criticism is symbolized by the piece of cloth that Saul is left with when he grabs at Samuel. The cloth, like all things Saul considers important, is man-made. The war song of the Israelite women, which ignites Saul's fury, further highlights Saul's flaw: "Saul has killed his thousands, / and David his ten thousands" (18:7). The refrain, which is repeated throughout the Book of Samuel by both priests and Philistines, illustrates the fact that Saul evaluates his leadership by human standards, rather than religious standards.

In contrast, God favors David because David places a higher value on religious devotion than on the physical world. David's inner virtue is Samuel's criterion for anointing him as king, and the encounter with Goliath functions as a parable for the triumph of the spiritual over the physical. The giant, a symbol of brute human force, is defeated by the diminutive David, who refuses the physical protection of the king's armor in favor of prayer, calling down God's wrath on the irreverent Goliath. David's repudiation of the physical world continues in his willingness to roam the desert on the margins of Israel, denying the opportunity to take the throne by physical force from God's current anointed ruler. Like Abraham and Moses, David reinforces God's ongoing preference for the unseen over the seen, the lesser over the greater, and inner faith over external circumstances. A commitment to these preferences seems to be the minimum religious requirement for the ideal Israelite monarch.

THE SECOND BOOK OF SAMUEL

SUMMARY

Upon learning of Saul's defeat by the Philistines, David sings a song lamenting the deaths of Saul and his friend, Jonathan. David goes to Hebron, where his followers and the southern tribe of Judah anoint him as king. Meanwhile, Saul's chief commander, Abner, garners the support of the northern tribes and instates Saul's son, Ish-Bosheth, as king of Israel. A war ensues between the conflicting regimes, played out in a series of small hand-to-hand contests between Abner's men and the army of Joab, David's general.

When Ish-Bosheth falsely accuses Abner of sleeping with one of the royal concubines, Abner defects to David's court. David welcomes Abner's support. Abner convinces the other tribes to recognize David's claim to the throne. Joab, however, seeks revenge for his brother's earlier death at Abner's hands, and he stabs Abner in secret. David's public censure of Joab and mourning for Abner wins Israel's respect, and two of Ish-Bosheth's men betray their ruler by presenting David with the severed head of the northern king. David is horrified that they have killed an innocent man, and he publicly executes these men. The united tribes declare David king of Israel.

David leads the Israelites in conquering the city of Jerusalem, a Canaanite stronghold lingering in the heart of Israel's territory. He erects his palace there and calls it "The City of David" or "Zion." Growing in power, David quells the ever-present Philistine threat in a decisive military victory. With the help of thirty thousand Israelites, David brings the Ark of the Covenant to Jerusalem in an elaborate procession. Amidst shouting and music, David dances and leaps in front of the Ark, to the embarrassment of his wife Michal. David rebukes her, claiming that he will humiliate himself as much as he wants so long as it pleases God. God is pleased that David has made a permanent home for the Ark and reveals a message to David's prophet, Nathan. God vows to grant Israel rest from foreign opposition and promises that the kingdom of David will last forever. With Joab's services, David subdues the nations of the surrounding area, expanding Israel's borders while developing diplomatic relations with the neighboring kingdoms.

One day, David watches a woman bathing from the rooftop of his palace. He summons the woman, Bathsheba, and has sex with her, and the woman becomes pregnant. Unable to disguise his indiscretion, David sends her husband, Uriah, to die on the battlefield. David marries Bathsheba, but Nathan confronts the king about his wrongdoing. Nathan tells a parable about a wealthy man who steals a poor man's only prized sheep. David is outraged by such selfishness, and Nathan informs David that the parable is about him. Nathan predicts that God will bring calamity on David's household. David repents for his wrongdoing, but, despite his fasting and praying, Bathsheba's son dies during childbirth. Afterward, David and Bathsheba have another son, Solomon.

David's older son Amnon falls in love with his half-sister Tamar and rapes her. David is furious but does nothing. Instead, Tamar's brother Absalom invites Amnon out to the country, where he and David's other sons murder Amnon. Absalom flees to a remote city for three years, but David, after mourning for Amnon, allows his son Absalom back to Jerusalem.

Absalom plots a conspiracy, forming an army and winning the hearts of the Israelite people through displays of warmth and kindness. Supported by David's chief counselor, Absalom goes to Hebron where his followers pronounce him king. Informed of this event, David flees from Jerusalem with his men, and the people of the countryside weep as he marches by. One of Saul's relatives, however, curses and throws stones at the band, gloating over David's demise. David forbids his attendants to punish the man.

Absalom enters Jerusalem where, in a display of defiance, he has sex with David's concubines. Absalom's aides advise him to attack David immediately, but one of David's officials, pretending to support Absalom, persuades Absalom to wait. This delay gives David time to muster an army, and his forces kill twenty thousand of Absalom's followers in the forests of Ephraim. Riding along, Absalom catches his head in the branches of a tree. Joab ignores David's instructions to treat Absalom gently and drives three spears into Absalom's hanging body. When David is notified of Absalom's death, he weeps, screaming repeatedly, "O my son Absalom, O Absalom, my son, my son!" (19:4).

To the frustration of his officials, David shows mercy to all of Absalom's supporters who approach him for forgiveness, especially Absalom's commander Amasa. David sends messengers to the leaders of Judah, and the tribe welcomes him back to Jerusalem. The remaining tribes—Absalom's chief supporters— fear that David will be angry at them. An uprising ensues, but Joab traps the rebels in a city and the city's residents hand over the severed head of the rebel leader. Angered that David has shown mercy to Amasa, Joab stabs Amasa one day while pretending to greet him.

David rebuilds his throne with continued acts of local diplomacy and with military victories over the Philistines. He composes a song praising God as a loving and kind deliverer, and the narrator briefly recounts the feats of David's most famous fighting men.

ANALYSIS

The major scholarly debate over 2 Samuel involves whether or not the book describes David in a negative or positive light. Chapters 9–20 of 2 Samuel are not necessarily complimentary. David commits adultery, tries to have his mistress's husband killed, and loses control of his sons. At the same time, however, the narrator explains how each of these incidents actually proves David's righteousness. Not only are David's sons blamed for their own actions, but David's own repentance for his misdeeds is described as exemplary. The circumstances surrounding David's reign suggest that God approves of David's actions. David's kingdom in Zion represents the fulfillment of God's promises to Abraham, Jacob, and Moses. It establishes the unified tribes of Israel in the promised land under the rule of a divinely sanctioned leader. David's triumphal entry into Jerusalem with the Ark of the Covenant marks the story's climax, symbolizing the ideal combination of religion and politics in Israel and the peaceful unification of God and man in one city. The image of an organized procession of song and dance around a symbol of God suggests that the people have, temporarily, reconciled their earthly aspirations with their religious commitments. 2 Samuel is characterized by the contrast between joyful images and images of civil conflict and confusion. All of the challengers to David's throne in Samuel lose their heads, symbolizing their thwarted attempts to become the head of Israel. David's retreat from Jerusalem to the sound of weeping and cursing contrasts with his earlier celebratory march into the city. Geographical motifs further reinforce this sense of division and loss. Ish-Bosheth's challenge to the throne divides Israel into two halves, northern and southern. Absalom is declared king outside of Jerusalem in Hebron, a symbol of his dissent from David, while his exhibition at the top of the palace represents his ascent to power. David, meanwhile, must move out from the center of Israel and across the Jordan River—the chief mark of one's exile from the promised land.

Individual characters express differing opinions about David's method of ruling. In one sense, David's mercy shows great prudence, for his tolerance of Ish-Bosheth eventually earns the respect of Ish-Bosheth's subjects. However, David's reluctance to punish Amnon for the rape of Tamar seems more permissive than just, and only fosters Absalom's rage. Joab similarly believes that David's kindness to Abner and Amasa is the result of oversight. Joab's decision to take matters into his own hands makes Joab a foil to David. While Joab is suspicious of others and concerned with end results, David is trusting and believes that an earnest response in the present moment is more important than outcomes. David's trust in the impulses of the present moment is the source of his greatest failing, his lust for Bathsheba. David's immediate impulses are also the source of the narrative's greatest moment of pathos—David's desperate cries for Absalom. Nevertheless, his mercy stabilizes Israel by providing second chances, not only to political rebels, but to some of the nation's most intriguing characters, such as Saul's cursing relative.

THE FIRST AND SECOND BOOKS OF KINGS

SUMMARY

David is old and bed-ridden, and his son Adonijah proclaims himself king with the help of David's commander Joab and the priest, Abiathar. Hearing this news, David instructs the prophet Nathan to anoint David's son, Solomon, as king. The people rally behind Solomon in a grand procession to the royal throne. Before dying, David charges Solomon to remain faithful to God and his laws. Solomon solidifies his claim to the throne by killing Joab,

Adonijah, and the remaining dissenters from David's reign. He also makes an alliance with Egypt by marrying the pharaoh's daughter.

Because Solomon carefully obeys God's laws, God appears to him in a dream and offers to grant the new king one wish. Solomon asks for wisdom to govern with justice and to know the difference between right and wrong. God is so impressed with Solomon's humble request that he promises Solomon the additional gifts of wealth and long life. As a result, Solomon lives in great opulence and his empire stretches from Egypt to the Euphrates River. He earns international fame for his wise sayings and scientific knowledge.

With his vast resources, Solomon builds an elaborate temple to God as well as a palace for himself in Jerusalem. Construction begins exactly four hundred and eighty years after Israel's exodus from Egypt. Solomon conscripts thousands of laborers for the work and imports materials from neighboring countries. The Temple is lined with gold and features large, hand-sculpted angels and pillars. Solomon places the Ark of the Covenant inside, and all of Israel gathers for the dedication. After sacrificing herds of animals on the altar, Solomon prays for God's blessing on the Temple. God appears to Solomon and promises to dwell in the Temple so long as Solomon and the Israelites are obedient to his laws. If they are not, God will remove his presence from the Temple, destroying both the temple and the nation.

Solomon's success continues until he marries many foreign women. They influence him to worship and erect altars to foreign deities. God is infuriated and tells Solomon that he will dismember the kingdom. God will tear away all of the tribes from Solomon's kingdom except for one, Judah. God allows the tribe of Judah to remain since Solomon is David's son. Following God's declaration, a prophet meets one of Solomon's officials, Jeroboam, with a cloak torn into twelve pieces, representing the twelve tribes of Israel. The prophet hands Jeroboam ten of the twelve pieces and explains that God has chosen him to rule these selected tribes as Israel's new king.

Solomon dies, and his son Rehoboam assumes the throne. Led by Jeroboam, the people gather before the young king to request that Rehoboam treat them more kindly than Solomon did during his reign. Rehoboam is headstrong and refuses, threatening to punish and enslave the people. The Israelites unite in rebellion, cursing the tribe of Judah and eluding Rehoboam's attempts to forcefully subdue them. They head north, where they crown Jeroboam king of Israel in the city of Shechem. Israel splits into two kingdoms: the kingdom of Israel in the north, and the kingdom of Judah in the south.

To distinguish the new, separate kingdom of Israel from the old kingdom in Jerusalem, Jeroboam erects altars and shrines to golden calves throughout the northern land. The Israelites worship the idols, and the Levite priests, formerly devoted to God, serve them as well. One day, Jeroboam's son is ill, and his wife approaches a prophet to seek guidance. The prophet warns that Jeroboam's household will be destroyed and that Israel will eventually lose control of the promised land because of Jeroboam's abhorrent practices. One generation later, Jeroboam's entire family is slaughtered when another Israelite takes the throne by force.

Meanwhile, King Rehoboam also erects altars and shrines to idols in Judah, even authorizing male and female prostitution in these shrines. The two kingdoms, northern and southern, continue to fight each other. After Rehoboam and Jeroboam die, the narrator recounts the story of all the succeeding kings in each kingdom, summarizing each king's reign by whether he does good or evil. Almost all of Israel's northern kings commit great evil, expanding on the practices of their fathers. Some of the southern kings in Jerusalem try to revive obedience to God, but none of them bans the worship of foreign gods in Judah.

With the help of his wife Jezebel, Ahab, northern Israel's most wicked king, spreads cult worship of the god Baal throughout the northern lands. In response, a prophet named Elijah emerges and informs Ahab that God will curse the land with a great drought. Elijah leads a secluded life on the outskirts of civilization. Ravens bring Elijah food and he performs miracles for the local people. After three years of drought, Queen Jezebel begins a campaign to murder all of God's prophets in the land. Elijah publicly confronts Ahab, demanding that the Israelite people profess allegiance to either God or Baal. The people do not respond. Elijah challenges the priests of Baal to a contest to see whose god can miraculously set an unlit animal sacrifice on fire. Despite animated prayer and self-mutilation, the priests of Baal are unable to ignite their altar. Elijah soaks his altar in water three times, and, when he prays, God engulfs the altar in flames.

Elijah flees from the belligerent Jezebel into the desert. He complains to God that, despite his earnest service, the Israelites continue to be disobedient. God promises to show himself to Elijah. Elijah is surrounded by wind, earthquakes, and fire, but none of these, we are told, is God. Instead, Elijah hears a soft whisper amidst the storm, and he recognizes that this is God. Encouraged, Elijah returns to civilization where he appoints a new man, Elisha, to be his apprentice and to eventually succeed him as prophet.

One day, Ahab and Jezebel steal a man's vineyard by slandering the man's name in public until the citizens stone the man. Elijah finds Ahab in the vineyard and declares that because of their murderous deeds, Ahab and Jezebel will die and dogs will lick up their blood. Soon after, King Ahab makes a rare pact with the king of Judah. The two lead their united forces against the Arameans who are occupying Israel's borders. Ahab is killed and bleeds to death in his chariot. When the chariot is cleaned after battle, dogs gather to lick his blood.

Not long after, Elijah is miraculously taken up into heaven by a flaming chariot, never to return, while Elisha looks on. Elisha assumes Elijah's role as prophet, acting as a cryptic doomsayer to Israel's kings while performing miracles for the common folk. Elisha helps a barren woman become pregnant, and when her young son suddenly dies, Elisha brings the boy back to life by lying on top of him. He guides the king of Israel in eluding the Aramean invaders from the north by plaguing the enemy troops with blindness.

Elisha initiates a coup to cut off Ahab and Jezebel's dynasty by secretly anointing a military commander, Jehu, to overthrow the throne. Jehu descends on the city where the current king, who is Ahab's son, and Judah's king are visiting each other. The men of the city rapidly defect to Jehu's side. Jehu overcomes the kings on horseback and shoots them with an arrow, decrying their witchcraft and idolatry in the process. Entering the city, Jezebel calls out seductively to Jehu from a window. The men of the city throw her out the window, and Jehu's horses trample her. The dogs eat her dead body, fulfilling Elijah's prophecy. After killing the rest of Ahab's family, Jehu invites all the priests of Baal to an assembly and murders them. He wipes out the Baal cult in Israel, but he does not forbid the worship of other gods.

The narrator continues the chronological account of Israel and Judah's kings. Each of Israel's kings is more evil than the previous, and Northern Israel gradually loses its territories to Assyrian pressure from the northeast. Assyria finally invades the northern kingdom of Israel entirely and captures the Israelites, removing them to Assyria. God's presence leaves the people of Israel, and scattered Near-Eastern groups populate the promised land, worshipping their own gods.

A handful of Judah's kings make a brave attempt at reform in the southern kingdom. Two kings embark on repairing the decaying Temple in Jerusalem. When Hezekiah assumes the throne, he destroys all of the altars and idols in Judah—the first such policy since Rehoboam introduced the idols into the land. With the help of the great prophet Isaiah, Judah thwarts heavy economic and military threats from Assyria. Finally, Judah's king Josiah directs a national program of spiritual renewal. He reads the Laws of Moses in front of all the people, and the people reaffirm their commitment to God's covenant, celebrating the Passover for the first time in centuries. Despite these attempts to turn the religious tide in Judah, however, evil rulers regain power after Josiah's death. The king of Babylon invades the southern kingdom of Israel, burning Jerusalem and destroying the Temple. Like their northern brothers, the people of Judah are exiled, settling in Babylon far away from their homeland.

ANALYSIS

The two volumes of Kings continue the story of Israel's tumultuous monarchy begun in Genesis and continued in the books of Samuel. The history spans almost four hundred years of events in ancient Israel. From the beginning of Solomon's reign in around 965 B.C. to the fall of the northern and southern kingdoms in 722 B.C. and 567 B.C., respectively, the nation of Israel dominates the international affairs of the Near East. As a result, many of the events described in the biblical account of Israel's divided kingdom can be authenticated historically. However, the authors of Kings do not simply list Israel and Judah's kings, but arrange their stories in a way that highlights the direct connection between Israel's religious infidelity and its radical political demise.

Solomon's temple is a monolithic symbol that changes to reflect the changing fortunes of the Israelites. The author interprets the temple's construction as a sign that Israel, the land originally promised to Moses, has arrived. By noting that Solomon builds it in "the four hundred and eightieth year after the Israelites came out of the land of Egypt," the narrator suggests that all of Israel's struggles to enter and conquer the promised land have prepared this moment (6:1). The Temple's large, solid structure is a physical manifestation of Israel's secure position in the land. God proves a spiritual manifestation of Israel's security when he promises to reside in the temple, placing his "name there forever" (9:3). The fact that the Temple is a man-made object that can decay foreshadows the eventual spiritual decay of Israel. Furthermore, the importance of a physical object to Solomon and the people contrasts with the importance in earlier biblical books of incorporeal spiritual elements. The temple also reflects the downfall of Israel. After the author spends four chapters detailing its construction and dedication, the Temple disappears from the narrative just as Israel's religious commitment to God fades from the minds of its rulers. Its final destruction at the hands of the Babylonians mirrors Israel's total neglect of God's covenant.

Part of the purpose of the books of Kings is to provide a cultural history of Israel that the Israelites can read to understand the history of their people. The authors and compilers of the books use rhetorical devices to reflect this purpose. One such device is the simultaneous telling of the histories of Israel and Judah. Accounts of Israelite kings always accompany accounts of contemporary kings in Judah. The narrator then describes how God views each king. This rhetorical device labels each king's reign as good or evil, and provides a moral evaluation of Israel and Judah's history. Judah appears generally more good than Israel since it has more good kings, a trend that reflects God's promise to Solomon that he will bless Judah because it is the site of King David's legacy in Jerusalem. On the whole, however, both Judah and Israel have a majority of evil kings. In spite of Hezekiah and Josiah's laudable reforms in Judah, the attacks by Assyria and Babylon appear to be punishment for the religious deterioration of the Israelites.

As the books' religious protagonists, Elijah and Elisha illustrate that the nature of prophets has changed throughout the Old Testament. Moses, Joshua, the judges, and David are all leaders of the Israelites, and, as the people's representatives, they meet with God on mountains or in religious centers to intercede on behalf of the people for their wrongdoing. Elijah and Elisha, however, are located on the outskirts of communities, and they utter mystical warnings or oracles to Israel that are fatalistic at best. Rather than leading the people to greatness, Elijah's contest with the priests of Baal is merely an attempt to diminish the people's ongoing evil, and Elisha's healing of the peasant boy only helps to ease pain. The narrator mentions Elisha's death only in passing, and Elijah is not actually buried in Israel. He is, instead, taken straight into heaven by supernatural means, an event that suggests that the land is too evil for God's prophets. Whereas God formerly presents himself to Moses using thunder and lightning, God's small, gentle whisper to Elijah shows that the people's worship of other deities has effectively quelled God's voice in Israel.

JOB

> *If I sin, what do I do to you, you watcher of*
> *humanity? Why have you made me your target?*
> (See QUOTATIONS, p. 109)

SUMMARY

Job is a wealthy man living in a land called Uz with his large family and extensive flocks. He is "blameless" and "upright," always careful to avoid doing evil (1:1). One day, Satan ("the Adversary") appears before God in heaven. God boasts to Satan about Job's goodness, but Satan argues that Job is only good because God has blessed him abundantly. Satan challenges God that, if given permission to punish the man, Job will turn and curse God. God allows Satan to torment Job to test this bold claim, but he forbids Satan to take Job's life in the process.

In the course of one day, Job receives four messages, each bearing separate news that his livestock, servants, and ten children have all died due to marauding invaders or natural catastrophes. Job tears his clothes and shaves his head in mourning, but he still blesses God in his prayers. Satan appears in heaven again, and God grants him another chance to test Job. This time, Job is afflicted with horrible skin sores. His wife encourages him to curse God and to give up and die, but Job refuses, struggling to accept his circumstances.

Three of Job's friends, Eliphaz, Bildad, and Zophar, come to visit him, sitting with Job in silence for seven days out of respect for his mourning. On the seventh day, Job speaks, beginning a conversation in which each of the four men shares his thoughts on Job's afflictions in long, poetic statements.

Job curses the day he was born, comparing life and death to light and darkness. He wishes that his birth had been shrouded in darkness and longs to have never been born, feeling that light, or life, only intensifies his misery. Eliphaz responds that Job, who has comforted other people, now shows that he never really understood their pain. Eliphaz believes that Job's agony must be due to some sin Job has committed, and he urges Job to seek God's favor. Bildad and Zophar agree that Job must have committed evil to offend God's justice and argue that he should strive to exhibit more blameless behavior. Bildad surmises that Job's children brought their deaths upon themselves. Even worse, Zophar implies that whatever wrong Job has done probably deserves greater punishment than what he has received.

Job responds to each of these remarks, growing so irritated that he calls his friends "worthless physicians" who "whitewash [their advice] with lies" (13:4). After making pains to assert his blameless character, Job ponders man's relationship to God. He wonders why God judges people by their actions if God can just as easily alter or forgive their behavior. It is also unclear to Job how a human can appease or court God's justice. God is unseen, and his ways are inscrutable and beyond human understanding. Moreover, humans cannot possibly persuade God with their words. God cannot be deceived, and Job admits that he does not even understand himself well enough to effectively plead his case to God. Job wishes for someone who can mediate between himself and God, or for God to send him to Sheol, the deep place of the dead.

Job's friends are offended that he scorns their wisdom. They think his questions are crafty and lack an appropriate fear of God, and they use many analogies and metaphors to stress their ongoing point that nothing good comes of wickedness. Job sustains his confidence in spite of these criticisms, responding that even if he has done evil, it is his own personal problem. Furthermore, he believes that there is a "witness" or a "Redeemer" in heaven who will vouch for his innocence (16:19, 19:25). After a while, the upbraiding proves too much for Job, and he grows sarcastic, impatient, and afraid. He laments the injustice that God lets wicked people prosper while he and countless other innocent people suffer. Job wants to confront God and complain, but he cannot physically find God to do it. He feels that wisdom is hidden from human minds, but he resolves to persist in pursuing wisdom by fearing God and avoiding evil.

Without provocation, another friend, Elihu, suddenly enters the conversation. The young Elihu believes that Job has spent too much energy vindicating himself rather than God. Elihu explains to Job that God communicates with humans by two ways—visions and physical pain. He says that physical suffering provides the sufferer with an opportunity to realize God's love and forgiveness when he is well again, understanding that God has "ransomed" him from an impending death (33:24). Elihu also assumes that Job must be wicked to be suffering as he is, and he thinks that Job's excessive talking is an act of rebellion against God.

God finally interrupts, calling from a whirlwind and demanding Job to be brave and respond to his questions. God's questions are rhetorical, intending to show how little Job knows about creation and how much power God alone has. God describes many detailed aspects of his creation, praising especially his creation of two large beasts, the Behemoth and Leviathan. Overwhelmed by the encounter, Job acknowledges God's unlimited power and admits the limitations of his human knowledge. This response pleases God, but he is upset with Eliphaz, Bildad, and Zophar for spouting poor and theologically unsound advice. Job intercedes on their behalf, and God forgives them. God returns Job's health, providing him with twice as much property as before, new children, and an extremely long life.

ANALYSIS

The Book of Job is one of the most celebrated pieces of biblical literature, not only because it explores some of the most profound questions humans ask about their lives, but also because it is extremely well written. The work combines two literary forms, framing forty chapters of verse between two and a half chapters of prose at the beginning and the end. The poetic discourse of

Job and his friends is unique in its own right. The lengthy conversation has the unified voice and consistent style of poetry, but it is a dialogue between characters who alter their moods, question their motives, change their minds, and undercut each other with sarcasm and innuendo. Although Job comes closest to doing so, no single character articulates one true or authoritative opinion. Each speaker has his own flaws as well as his own lofty moments of observation or astute theological insight.

The interaction between Job and his friends illustrates the painful irony of his situation. Our knowledge that Job's punishment is the result of a contest between God and Satan contrasts with Job's confusion and his friends' lecturing, as they try to understand why Job is being punished. The premise of the friends' argument is that misfortune only follows from evil deeds. Bildad instructs Job, "if you are pure and upright, / surely then [God] will rouse himself / for you" and he later goads Job to be a "blameless person" (8:6, 8:20). The language in these passages is ironic, since, unbeknownst to Job or Job's friends, God and Satan do in fact view Job as "blameless and upright." This contrast shows the folly of the three friends who ignore Job's pain while purporting to encourage him. The interaction also shows the folly of trying to understand God's ways. The three friends and Job have a serious theological conversation about a situation that actually is simply a game between God and Satan. The fault of Job and his friends lies in trying to explain the nature of God with only the limited information available to human knowledge, as God himself notes when he roars from the whirlwind, "Who is this that darkness counsel / by words without / knowledge?" (38:2).

The dominant theme of Job is the difficulty of understanding why an all-powerful God allows good people to suffer. Job wants to find a way to justify God's actions, but he cannot understand why there are evil people who "harm the childless woman, / and do no good to the widow," only to be rewarded with long, successful lives (24:21). Job's friends, including Elihu, say that God distributes outcomes to each person as his or her actions deserve. As a result of this belief, they insist that Job has committed some wrongdoing to merit his punishment. God himself declines to present a rational explanation for the unfair distribution of blessings among men. He boasts to Job, "Have you comprehended the / expanse of the earth? / Declare, if you know all this" (38:18). God suggests that people should not discuss divine justice since God's power is so great that humans cannot possibly justify his ways.

One of the chief virtues of the poetry in Job is its rhetoric. The book's rhetorical language seeks to produce an effect in the listener rather than communicate a literal idea. God's onslaught of rhetorical questions to Job, asking if Job can perform the same things he can do, overwhelms both Job and the reader with the sense of God's extensive power as well as his pride. Sarcasm is also a frequent rhetorical tool for Job and his friends in their conversation. After Bildad lectures Job about human wisdom, Job sneers, "How you have helped one / who has no power! / How you have assisted the arm / that has no strength!" (26:2). Job is saying that he already knows what Bildad has just explained about wisdom. The self-deprecating tone and sarcastic response are rare elements in ancient verse. Such irony not only heightens the playfulness of the text but suggests the characters are actively responding to each other, thus connecting their seemingly disparate speeches together. The poetry in Job is a true dialogue, for the characters develop ideas and unique personalities throughout the course of their responses.

ECCLESIASTES

> *For everything there is a season, and a time for*
> *every matter under heaven: a time to be born, and*
> *a time to die.... (See* QUOTATIONS, *p. 109)*

SUMMARY

The narrator of Ecclesiastes is a nameless person who calls himself a "Teacher," and identifies himself as the current king of Israel and a son of King David. The Teacher opens with the exclamation, "Vanity of vanities . . . ! All is vanity" (1:2). He laments that everything in life is endless and meaningless—especially human toil and the cycles of nature—for nothing is ever truly new on earth. As the wisest man in Jerusalem, the Teacher feels he is cursed with the unhappy task of discerning wisdom, for he has seen "all the deeds that are done under the sun" (1:14). In a mixture of prose and verse, the Teacher compiles his studies, hypotheses, and proverbs regarding wisdom.

The Teacher tries many earthly pleasures. He drinks, becomes wealthy, acquires power, buys property, experiences sexual gratification, and views artistic entertainment. However, none of these experiences satisfies him. Although the Teacher originally assumes that wisdom is better than folly, he realizes that achieving wisdom is a frustrating and elusive pursuit, for the wise and the foolish both die the same death. He hypothesizes that the best humans can do is to honor God and to eat, drink, and enjoy themselves.

The Teacher also surveys the general trends of human activity. He notes that just as there is time for each good thing in life, such as birth or love, there is always a time for its opposite, such as death or hate. It is often hard for mortal humans to understand the difference between wickedness and justice, but God distinguishes between the two. The Teacher notes that human labor is marked by competition, envy, and oppression. The Teacher praises the virtues of human cooperation, noting the advantages that a team of two or three individuals has over one person alone.

Next, the Teacher discusses various foolish actions, such as gluttony, the love of money, and excessive talking. The Teacher provides a series of instructions for avoiding such foolhardiness. Each saying extols negative experiences over positive ones: mourning, he claims, is better than feasting, and the end of things is better than the beginning. He also encourages people to be neither too righteous nor too wicked but to remain moderate.

Still, the Teacher remains bothered by the fact that both evil and good people meet the same fate. He grows tired of discussing the distinctions between good and bad, clean and unclean, obedient and disobedient. He ultimately decides that the only factors in determining the outcome between life's opposing forces are time and chance.

The Teacher gives positive exhortations. He encourages humans to enjoy their vain lives and activities to the fullest. People must embrace the unforeseen chances of life, since caution only impedes God's providence. He urges young people to remain happy and to follow their inclinations, reminding them to always remember God. The things of earth are only temporary, and life is a cycle that eventually returns to God (12:7). The Teacher also warns the reader against heeding too many wise sayings, for the study of wisdom never ends. The "end of the matter," he concludes, is for humans to fear God and to obey his commandments (12:13).

ANALYSIS

The Book of Ecclesiastes is a notoriously confusing portion of the Old Testament. The Teacher is uncertain and ambiguous in his writing. His claims suggest that the Teacher is the great King

Solomon—the son of King David whom God blesses with powers of immense wisdom. While this identity lends credibility to the book, the Teacher's comments are not at all systematic. The book is often repetitive or contradictory. The frequent changes in tone make it unclear whether the Teacher intends his comments to describe how humans naturally behave or to tell people how they should behave. The Teacher's recurring lament of "vanity" is emblematic of the book's elusive intentions. "Vanity" is a translation of the Hebrew word hebel, which means "breath of the wind," connoting uselessness, deceptiveness, and transience. Indeed, the Teacher's confusing style may be a means to reinforce his argument that human wisdom is essentially limited or "vain."

Ecclesiastes' manner of teaching contrasts with the rest of the Old Testament because it questions the process of receiving wisdom and ideals. Although much of the Old Testament is aimed at setting up absolute opposites, The Teacher is skeptical of such binary opposites. He does not endorse the division of the world into positive and negative forces, including good and evil, peace and war, clean and unclean. The Teacher does not believe that these forces do not exist, but he suggests that defining life within such simplistic terms may not be an effective way for human beings to understand it. In his most famous verse, he notes that each experience has its appropriate place in life: there is "a time to keep silence, and a time / to speak; / a time to love, and a time to hate . . ." (3:7–8). This verse suggests that the tension between positive and negative experiences is fundamental to human life, and that only God can truly judge when a situation is either good or evil. Later, he assumes a more pessimistic tone, affirming that time and chance are the only determining factors in the race between good and evil. The premise of this point of view is that the difference between good and evil is so subtle and transient that humans cannot confidently assume they are able to differentiate between good and evil or between obedience and disobedience.

The Teacher's mode of argument is consistent with his beliefs about the limitations of human reason. Rather than providing us with a set of general rules or guidelines for wise behavior, the Teacher makes a series of observations about concrete human experiences. The Teacher's study of human pleasure is empirical, testing each pleasurable experience and forming conclusions only on the basis of observations. The Teacher also refers to what he sees or finds in life rather than what he thinks. He says, "See, this is what I found . . . adding one thing to another to find the sum, which my mind has sought repeatedly, but I have not found" (7:27). The "sum," or final meaning, of human life eludes the Teacher, and he prefers to base his thoughts on his experiences. The Teacher's proverbs and sayings focus on concrete objects and feelings. To encourage humans to embrace life's chances, he instructs, "Send out your bread upon the waters . . ." (11:1). He also speaks about walking on the road, charming snakes, digging pits, looking at the sun, and, as always, his chief advice is to eat, drink, and be merry. These sayings are metaphors and symbols for diverse experiences from which larger conclusions can be drawn; but the Teacher leaves the interpretation of his sayings to the reader, further emphasizing his distaste for rigid or dogmatic wisdom.

Psalms

Overview

A psalm is a religious poem or song set to music. Some of the psalms in the Book of Psalms are hymns to be sung by a congregation, and "Songs of Ascent" to be sung by pilgrims approaching the Temple.

Some are private prayers, and some are lyrical devices for recalling historical events in Israel's history. In its current form, the Book of Psalms contains one hundred and fifty individual psalms, although this number may vary in different biblical translations.

Traditionally, the psalms are separated into five books, and many poems are further distinguished by brief titles attributing the given work to a specific author, though these titles were probably added at a later date by an editor or group of editors of the psalms; the authorship of the psalms is uncertain at best. Because the subject matter of the psalms ranges from the events of King David's dynasty to the exile of the Israelites in Babylon, the poems may have been composed anywhere from the tenth century B.C. to the sixth century B.C. or later.

Many of the psalms rehearse episodes of Israel's history, especially the story of Israel's exodus from Egypt and its arrival in the promised land. Psalm 137 is a beautiful lament of the early days of Israel's captivity in Babylon. The poem opens with the image of the Israelites weeping by the banks of the Babylonian rivers, longing for Jerusalem, or Zion. When their captors ask the Israelites to sing for them, the Israelites refuse, hanging their harps on the branches of the willow trees. The poet asks, "How could we sing the Lord's / song / in a foreign land?" (137:4). The poem ends with a call for vengeance on the Babylonians. It acts as an earnest reminder both to the exiled Israelites and to later biblical readers of the importance of the promised land for the celebration of the Jewish faith.

TYPES OF PSALMS
A majority of the biblical psalms are devoted to expressing praise or thanksgiving to God. Psalm 8, for instance, is a communal or public declaration of praise to God for his relationship with creation. The poet praises God for his command over each level

of creation, beginning with the cosmos, then descending gradually to humankind, the animals, and, lastly, the sea. The speaker expresses amazement that God, who is above the heavens, not only concerns himself with the welfare of humans but places humans directly beneath himself in importance, granting them authority over the rest of creation, which is "under their feet" (8:6). Poems such as Psalm 46 praise "the city of God" or "Zion" for being God's home, and many of the psalms suggest a grand entrance to Jerusalem, such as Psalm 100: "Enter his gates with thanksgiving, / and his courts with praise" (100:4). Similarly, when the speaker says in Psalm 121, "I lift my eyes to the hills," the poem conveys the expectation and longing of the Jewish worshipper as he approaches the Temple in Jerusalem (121:1).

Another category of psalms includes laments or supplications, poems in which the author requests relief from his physical suffering and his enemies. These enemies may be actual, such as opposing nations or public accusers, or they may be figurative depictions of an encroaching spiritual evil. In Psalm 22, the speaker characterizes the band of nondescript evildoers that trouble the poet as a series of approaching ravenous animals—first bulls, then roaring lions, and then dogs. The evildoers surround the speaker, staring at and gloating over his now shriveled and emaciated body, finally stripping him of his clothes. In verse nineteen, the speaker cries for God's relief, and God proceeds to deliver him from each of the three beasts in reverse order—first from the dog, then from the lion, and finally from the wild oxen. God's sudden rescue complete, the psalm of lament becomes a psalm of thanksgiving as the speaker vows to announce God's praises to all of Israel.

Supplication and lament are integral parts of another type of psalm, in which the poet moves from despair over his own wrongdoing to a profession of deeper faith in God. These are some of the most beloved psalms, for they are deeply personal poems that offer hope of redemption for the individual. The poet decries his spiritual despair using metaphors similar to the psalms of lament. In Psalm 40, the poet is stuck in a "desolate / pit" and a "miry bog" until God sets him "upon a rock" (40:2). The poet walks through dark valleys in Psalm 23, his body wastes away in Psalm 32, and his bones are crushed in Psalm 51. God relieves the poet by acting as a "refuge," a "strong fortress," and a "hiding place" (31:2, 32:7).

Psalms devoted to wisdom use proverbs or catchy rhetorical devices to give moral instructions to the reader. For example, Psalm 127 opens with a quaint proverb to encourage the listener's devotion to God: "Unless the Lord builds the house, / those who build it labor in vain" (127:1). Psalm 119, the longest psalm in the Bible with 176 verses, is a meditation on God's law using an acrostic—a poem in which each segment begins with a consecutive letter of the Hebrew alphabet.

POETIC FORM AND STYLE

The poet of Psalms consistently uses parallelism to enhance his meaning. Unlike Roman poetry, in which rhythm and meter are structured around a pattern of stressed syllables, biblical poetry is largely based on pairings of "versets"—segments or halves of verses and lines, usually only a handful of words long. These versets "parallel" each other, the second verset reiterating or expanding upon the ideas of the first verset. Sometimes, parallel versets repeat the same words:

> *The voice of the Lord breaks the cedars;*
> *the Lord breaks the cedars of Lebanon.* *(29:5)*

More often, however, parallel versets repeat meaning. In Psalm 40:8, the speaker says,

> *I delight to do your will, O my God;*
> *your law is within my heart.*   *(40:8)*

Here, the poet restates that obedience to God is very important to him. The second line, however, offers the reader new and more specific information, affirming, in figurative language, that God's commandments are so precious to the speaker that they reside in his heart. In this way, the parallelism of meaning in biblical poetry is not just a system of redundant lines. Rather, parallelism of meaning helps develop the imagery and ideas within each psalm by creating the occasion for analogies, greater detail, and showing how one event or idea follows from another.

Despite the sheer number and variety of the psalms, the metaphors throughout the one hundred and fifty poems are consistent. The poet's enemies are typically described as listless or transient creatures, usually wild animals or approaching natural catastrophes. Psalm 91 characterizes the speaker's enemies as "deadly pestilence," as well as lions and serpents, and Psalm 1 compares the wicked to chaff blowing in the wind. The poet or protagonist, on the other hand, is typically one who is lost or displaced. In Psalm 42, the poet refers to himself as a deer searching for flowing streams, and in other poems, the speaker is wandering on a dangerous path or stuck in a ditch or a bog. God, however, is frequently spoken of in geological or geographical terms. He is a rock, a refuge, and a fortress; he resides in the hills and, more importantly, in Zion, the city of Jerusalem. In a sense, God is himself a location, a "hiding place" in Psalm 32 and someone who draws "boundary lines" for the poet (16:6). Even as a shepherd in Psalm 23, God directs the wandering poet to "green pastures" and welcomes him to a table—a centralized location. These images of God as a place of protection that is somehow united with the land elaborate the promised land of the Old Testament as a symbol of Israel's religious well-being.

THE SONG OF SOLOMON

SUMMARY

The Song of Solomon is a series of lyrical poems organized as a lengthy dialogue between a young woman and her lover. A third party, or chorus, occasionally addresses the lovers. The first poem is spoken by the young maiden, who longs to be near her lover and enjoy his kisses. She explains that she has a dark complexion because her family sends her to work in the vineyards. She searches for her lover, comparing him to a wandering shepherd, and the chorus encourages her to follow the flocks to his tent.

The lovers lie on a couch together. The man praises the beauty of his beloved, comparing her to a young mare and comparing her eyes to doves' eyes. He describes verdant and fertile surroundings. The maiden calls herself a rose and a lily, covered by the shade of her beloved, a fruit tree. She compares her beloved to a lively gazelle that arrives to take her away during spring when the plants are budding. The maiden boasts that the man now pastures his flocks of sheep among her lilies. She warns other women, "the daughters of Jerusalem," not to fall in love too early (2:7).

While in bed, the maiden dreams that she is searching the city streets for her lover and that she finds him and takes him home. She envisions a lavish wedding procession, in which her happy bridegroom appears as King Solomon. The man speaks, comparing each part of the maiden's body to animals and precious objects. He calls for her to come down from the mountain peaks to be with him. With intense yearning, he characterizes her as an enclosed "garden" full of ripe foliage and a flowing fountain (4:12–15). The maiden bids the wind to blow on her garden and invites the man into the garden. The man dines in the garden and calls for their friends to celebrate with the lovers.

In another dream, the maiden hears her lover knocking at her door late one night, but he disappears. Again, she roams the streets, but this time the city guards accost the maiden. She asks the "daughters of Jerusalem" to help her find her lover. The chorus asks her to describe the young man, and she compares each part of his body to precious metals, jewels, and animals.

The two find each other in the garden. The man continues to praise each part of the maiden's body. He bids her to dance and likens her to a palm tree with breasts like fruit. The maiden invites her lover to the fields and villages, promising to give him her love among the blossoming vineyards. She wishes that he were her brother so that people would not comment about their open displays of affection. She urges him to "seal" his heart with her love, for love is strong. The maiden thinks back on her earlier chastity but is glad she has lost it peacefully "in his eyes" (8:10). The man says that, while King Solomon may have many vineyards, he is happy with his one vineyard, the maiden.

ANALYSIS

The Song of Solomon is also called "The Song of Songs," suggesting that it is the greatest of all songs. The first title implies that King Solomon composed the collection of love poems, but Solomon's name was probably added at a later date by the song's editors, perhaps because of references within the text to the wise and prolific king. This attribution to Solomon led to the book's inclusion in the

Hebrew Bible and later, Christian versions of the Old Testament. Early Hebrew and Christian scholars long maintained that the love story is an allegory of God's love for humankind, or of the intensity of divine love within the human heart. However, it is undeniable that the song celebrates not only human love but also the sensuous and mystical quality of erotic desire.

Modern scholars see similarities between The Song of Solomon and other ancient Near-Eastern stories in which the fertility of the earth depends upon the sexual encounter of a male and female deity. Although the biblical maiden and her lover themselves do not affect the fertility of the land, there are numerous parallels between the fertile vegetation of their surroundings and the success of their romance. The lovers recline on a green couch, whose color suggests a connection with nature. The song also explicitly compares the man and woman to vegetation: the woman is a flower and the man is a fruit tree. Images of plants and frolicking animals are symbols of life, and as such they are metaphors for the procreative act of human sexual relations. The song's references to spring and the budding of plants further emphasize the budding of romantic arousal. The couple always celebrates their love in such verdant environments—in the wilderness, the vineyard, or the garden. It is in the city, where plants do not grow and the city guards are brutal, that the maiden searches for her lover but cannot find him.

The man's comparison of the maiden to a "garden locked" and "fountain sealed" establishes the relationship between chastity and femininity (4:12). The image of an enclosed garden is a metaphor for female virginity that is frequently repeated in later medieval and Renaissance literature. In the Song of Solomon, the closed garden suggests that the girl is chaste and unsullied. The man's dining in the garden implies that the two have consummated their relationship, and his invitation to the chorus to celebrate this event with feasting further indicates the completion of this rite of passage. Later, the two walk in a vineyard, and the girl remembers her earlier virginity when she was cursed to labor in the vineyard instead of enjoying it. Her memory while in the vineyard suggests the bittersweet nature of the loss of innocence.

The garden motif is reminiscent of the Garden of Eden in Genesis, where Adam and Eve enjoy God's creation prior to the emergence of human wickedness. The parallels to Eden in The Song of Solomon suggest that the celebration of human sensuality is, itself, a good and not a wicked thing. The maiden and her lover, however, must enjoy their love within the boundaries and confines of gardens and fields. This limitation on the enjoyment of their sexual behavior is in keeping with the ongoing biblical theme that there are ethical requirements for enjoying God's promises—for Adam and Eve to remain in the garden of Eden and for the Israelites to dwell in the promised land.

PROVERBS

OVERVIEW

Proverbs is the chief volume in the biblical collection of wisdom literature, which also includes Ecclesiastes, Job, and portions of Psalms. The purpose of wisdom literature in the Bible is to teach rather than to relate a narrative. Proverbs contains thirty-one chapters, each comprised of twenty to thirty-five wise sayings that are each two poetic lines long. Most of the book is attributed to King Solomon; but, as the book itself indicates, the written teachings in their current form were probably collected no earlier than the reign of Hezekiah, King of Judah in the late eighth and early seventh centuries B.C.

Other sections of the text are attributed to additional, more obscure authors. However, it is safe to say that Proverbs represents the written record of an oral tradition of wise sayings with uncertain origins.

A proverb is a short, pithy saying that usually draws a comparison between two forms of behavior in order to impart moral or religious wisdom to its receiver. Some of the wise sayings in Proverbs also take the form of enigmatic or cryptic utterances that the receiver must interpret to understand the meaning. Biblical proverbs are religious, but they focus on concrete human experiences rather than divine revelation. Nevertheless, their judgments always entail a timeless quality, like the moral of a myth or a folktale. The biblical notion of wisdom implies acquiring skill or ability in the areas of justice and moral goodness—like a craftsmen learning a craft. In fact, Proverbs frequently instructs the listener to "get" or "buy" wisdom (4:5 and 23:23). The sayings in Proverbs are often addressed to young people, who are in the process of becoming wise. It is likely that the Book of Proverbs formed part of the education for Hebrew youth after the Israelite exile and return to the promised land.

STRUCTURE

The Book of Proverbs is divided into four main sections, with three additional sections, or appendices, included at the end. The first third of Proverbs is an extended lecture spoken by the personified voice of "Wisdom." This section is the most conversational, narrative, and thematic portion of the book. Wisdom speaks in the first person and refers to the reader as "my child," instructing the reader on various topics for wise living. The voice of Wisdom assumes different forms. On the one hand, Wisdom refers to itself in feminine terms, using the pronouns "she" and "her." Wisdom describes itself as a woman standing on the city streets, crying out her warnings to the people. However, Wisdom also identifies itself with God.

Pursuing Wisdom, it says, is the same thing as obeying God, and Wisdom claims to have been God's partner in creating the world.

The next three sections of Proverbs contain the proverbs of Solomon and the sayings of the wise. The list of Solomon's proverbs is made up of two lengthy sections, and the proverbs are very loosely organized by theme. The speaker usually assumes the voice and authority of a king. Many of the proverbs follow the formula of antithetical parallelism, a convention in which the proverb is stated in two poetic lines, and one line describes a type of good or wise behavior while the other describes its evil or foolish opposite. The "sayings of the wise" make up one small section and are less rhetorical, issuing more direct commands and advice to the reader.

The final three sections in Proverbs include the brief oracles of Agur and King Lemuel and a closing lesson on how to select a good wife. Agur and Lemuel's historical existence is unknown, but their cryptic sayings continue the demand for wisdom and the themes of temperance and justice that are common to the rest of Proverbs. The final passage praises all the traits of the good and "capable" wife (31:10). She is industrious, independent, strong, generous to the poor, and, most importantly, she "fears," or obeys, God (31:30). Proverbs closes by calling for her family and the community to praise her.

THEMES

Proverbs is largely concerned with the inevitability of God's justice and the importance of prudence and moderation. Solomon's proverbs maintain that wicked deeds will invariably lead to divine retribution and punishment during a person's earthly life. People who slander others will have their tongues cut off, those who are lazy will have failing crops, and undue pride will lead to an individual's downfall. One way to enjoy the favorable hand of God's justice is to practice moderation and prudence. According to the proverbs, the moderate person avoids the excesses of the foolish, including excessive drinking, eating, sleeping, gossiping, and rage. A consistent way to demonstrate wise behavior is by choosing words shrewdly and carefully. The proverbs also praise those who prepare in advance, particularly those who build their homes in preparation for later circumstances. The most important sign of wisdom and prudence, however, is obedience and reverence to one's parents.

The importance of women and femininity in Proverbs is unusual in the context of the Old Testament. In most Old Testament narratives, women play a role secondary to that of men. However, Proverbs suggests that women can use wisdom within a male-dominated society to assert their strength and independence. The final chapter gives license to the "good wife" to do everything from selling merchandise to performing home repair, and Solomon notes earlier that it is the "wise woman who builds her house" (14:1). Interestingly, the young men throughout Proverbs wander aimlessly, searching for the correct path but falling prey to seduction. Wisdom, personified as a woman, stands fast, stationed at the city gates or in the streets delivering messages as an oracle or sooth-sayer. The juxtaposition of feminine Wisdom with God alters the vision of God from previous biblical books, in which God appears as an angel, a group of men, or in thunder and fire. The Book of Proverbs does not suggest that God is a woman or a being with a gender. Nevertheless, the feminine voice of Wisdom claims to be an integral part of God. Wisdom notes, "The Lord created me at the / beginning of his work. . . . [T]hen I was beside him, like a / master worker" (8:22–30). Wisdom also affirms, "For whoever finds me finds life / and obtains favor from the Lord" (8:35). Wisdom is the source of life, a helper in creation, and a mediator between God and humankind. By assigning Wisdom a feminine quality, Proverbs suggests that femininity, in addition to masculinity, should be an important way in which we think about the order of the world.

Important Quotations Explained

1. I will make you exceedingly fruitful; and I will make nations of you, and kings shall come from you. I will establish my covenant between me and you, and your offspring after you throughout their generations, for an everlasting covenant, to be God to you and to your offspring after you. And I will give to you, and to your offspring after you, the land where you are now an alien, all the land of Canaan, for a perpetual holding; and I will be their God.

(Genesis 17:6–8)

These words, spoken by God, articulate God's covenant, or promise, with Abraham. Initially in the Genesis narrative, the interaction between God and humans seems bewildering and arbitrary. God speaks to isolated individuals and demands certain actions from them. Here, God lays out a plan for an ongoing relationship with humankind. God will be the deity of one group of people, and the rights to God's favor and blessings will pass on genetically from one man to his descendants. The rewards of this relationship will not only be a nation and a homeland for the Israelites but abundant, "fruitful" life. God's comments here serve two functions. First, the passage introduces the dominant motif of the Old Testament: the covenant unifies the biblical narrative, for everything the Israelites do from this point on represents either an affirmation or a rejection of God's promise. Second, the passage implies that the Israelites are not just any group or ethnicity, but a specific people descending from

QUOTATIONS

one man with a divine claim to land in the eastern Mediterranean region. Historically, the idea of the covenant was important for the Israelites in sustaining a sense of identity in the ethnic mix of the region as well as during the exile.

2.   Hear, O Israel: The Lord is our God, the Lord alone.
      You shall love the Lord your God with all your heart,
      and with all your soul, and with all your might. Keep
      these words that I am commanding you today in your
      heart. Recite them to your children and talk about them
      when you are at home and when you are away, when
      you lie down and when you rise. Bind them as a sign on
      your hand, fix them as an emblem on your forehead.
                                        (Deuteronomy 6:4–8)

Stationed on the border of the Promised Land, Moses delivers these instructions in his farewell address to the Israelites. In one sense, his speech, which constitutes the Book of Deuteronomy, is redundant. Moses reiterates many of the religious laws and commandments already stated by God in the Book of Leviticus and the latter half of Exodus. However, Moses is speaking to a new, younger generation of Israelites who, after wandering the desert for forty years, are now ready to take the land sworn to them by God, a land they have never seen. Just as the history of Israel is at a turning point, so Moses describes the laws and the covenant in terms very different than before. Previously, the symbols of God's covenant have been external: the rite of circumcision, the Ark of the Covenant, and various rules for physical cleanliness. Now, Moses describes the laws as internal to the Israelites. The religious laws are words and ideas that should be so precious to the Israelites that they are in their "heart[s]," remaining with the people wherever they go. This passage suggests why Judaism refers to the biblical laws as "Torah": laws that are not just rules for behavior but models for all of life.

3.   Has the Lord as great delight in burnt offerings and sacrifices, as in obedience to the voice of the Lord?
     Surely, to obey is better than sacrifice,
     and to heed than the fat of rams. . . .
     Because you have rejected the word of the Lord,
     he has also rejected you from being king.

                                                                    (1 Samuel 15:22–23)

The prophet Samuel pronounces this grim curse to Saul after Saul disobeys God. Through Samuel, God has instructed King Saul to attack the neighboring Amalekites and destroy them completely, sparing nothing. Saul, however, has brought back the Amalekite flocks as booty, apparently to use as a ritual animal sacrifice to God. This seemingly benign error not only earns God's wrath but justifies the removal of Saul as king of Israel. As such, the oversight marks a turning a point in the history of Israel, permitting David's ascent to the throne. More important, the nature of Saul's error implies a new outlook on religious obedience. Obedience is not adherence to God's laws but obedience to God himself. As Samuel suggests, God honors obedience to that which is unseen—"the voice of the Lord"—more than obedience to that which is seen—physical regulations and ceremonies. Valuing the unseen over the seen is integral to the theme of radical faith in the Old Testament. Saul does not possess this faith, yet his tragic demise over such a fine distinction earns our sympathy.

4.   If I sin, what do I do to you, you watcher of humanity?
     Why have you made me your target?
     Why have I become a burden to you?

                                                    (Job 7:20)

This rhetorical question is spoken by Job after God has killed all
his children and his livestock, and afflicted him with a skin disease.
Job's lament is emblematic of the central question discussed by Job
and his three friends. The question is a theme in the Old Testament:
how can God remain good despite the fact that he allows evil and
human suffering to exist? Job's friends argue that God would only
afflict Job with pain if he had committed some grave act of human
disobedience meriting punishment. Job, however, raises two
complaints against God, the "watcher of humanity." For one, Job
knows he has done nothing wrong, and he wonders what he could
have done to become a "burden" to God and deserve such suffering.
Second, Job asks why God is so concerned with human actions in
the first place—why he watches humanity's faults and punishes them
in turn. Just as Job's lament is rhetorical and open-ended, so this
question and theme is not explicitly answered in the Old Testament.

5.   For everything there is a season, and a
     time for every matter under heaven:
     a time to be born, and a time to die;
     a time to plant, and a time to pluck up what is planted;
     a time to kill, and a time to heal;
     a time to break down, and a time to build up;
     a time to weep, and a time to laugh;
     a time to mourn, and a time to dance. . . .

                                          (Ecclesiastes 3:1–4)

These famous verses are spoken by the unnamed Teacher who investigates the meaning of life in the Book of Ecclesiastes. The poetic interlude in the Teacher's musings represents an excellent example of the parallelism that defines biblical poetry: the lyrical verse has rhythm because each line is divided into two halves, both of which mirror and oppose each other at the same time. More important, the Teacher's saying continues the pattern of doubles and opposites developed throughout the Old Testament narrative. Since God's creation in Genesis, the Old Testament depicts the world as a place of opposing forces—good versus evil, greater versus lesser, light versus dark, seen versus unseen. The Old Testament frequently reverses these opposites, showing the younger dominating over the older, the weak over the strong, and the oppressed over the powerful. This motif suggests that humans cannot confidently discern that which is better or worse without faith in God. Similarly, the Teacher explains that there is a time for every human experience, good and bad. One cannot say that dancing is obviously better than mourning, for both experiences are integral to human life. The Teacher argues that trying to find meaning in life by what people traditionally assume to be better or worse is misguided, and that the only correct way for humans to behave is to fear, or obey, God.

REVIEW AND RESOURCES

QUIZ

1. Why does Cain kill his brother Abel?
   A. Because the serpent tells him to
   B. Because Abel teases Cain
   C. Because Adam loves Abel more
   D. Because God is more pleased by Abel's sacrifice than by Cain's

2. Which of the following is not a sign of God's covenant, or promise, with Abraham?
   A. The rite of circumcision
   B. God renaming Abraham and his wife Sarah
   C. God destroying the cities of Sodom and Gomorrah
   D. God providing Sarah with a son, Isaac

3. How does Jacob steal his brother Esau's inheritance rights?
   A. By killing his brother
   B. By tricking his father with the help of his mother
   C. By sleeping with his mother
   D. By exposing Esau's plan to murder his father

4. How many sons does Jacob have?
   A. Three
   B. Four
   C. Ten
   D. Twelve

5. What is Jacob's alternate name?
    A. Judah
    B. Isaac
    C. Israel
    D. Ishmael

6. From which catastrophe does Joseph save Egypt?
    A. Famine
    B. A plague
    C. Military invasion
    D. A flood

7. How does God first appear to Moses?
    A. As a group of three men
    B. As an angel
    C. As a flaming sword
    D. As a burning bush

8. What object that God gives Moses allows him to perform signs and wonders?
    A. The stone tablets
    B. A wooden staff
    C. A colorful robe
    D. A golden censer

9. How does God feed the Israelites in the desert?
    A. By miraculously providing fish from the Red Sea
    B. By a strange bread-like substance from heaven
    C. By food produced from Moses's staff
    D. By an endless supply of produce from Egypt

10. Why does Moses break the stone tablets inscribed with God's commandments at Mount Sinai?
    A. Because he trips walking down the mountain
    B. Because God commands him to
    C. Because Moses refuses to lead the people any longer
    D. Because the people are worshipping a golden idol

11. Why does God curse the Israelites to wander the desert for forty years before entering the promised land?
    A. Because a group of Israelite spies incites an uprising to return to Egypt
    B. Because the Israelites incorrectly perform the ritual sacrifice
    C. Because the Israelites vote down Moses as their leader
    D. Because the Israelites worship golden idols

12. What do Moses and Joshua forbid the Israelites to do in the promised land?
    A. Intermarry with the native inhabitants
    B. Conquer the cities of the region
    C. Divide the land amongst the twelve tribes
    D. Bathe in the Jordan River

13. Who betrays Samson to the Philistines?
    A. Sarah
    B. Delilah
    C. Gideon
    D. Deborah

14. Why does God reject Saul as king of Israel?
    A. Because Saul has too many concubines
    B. Because Saul kills Samuel
    C. Because Saul does not completely destroy the Amalekites
    D. Because Saul is too cowardly to fight the Philistines

15. Why does the prophet Nathan rebuke David?
    A. David fails to build the Temple to God.
    B. David curses God inadvertently.
    C. David commits adultery with Bathsheba.
    D. David allows one of his sons to rape his stepsister.

16. What does David bring to Jerusalem to bless the religious city?
    A. The body of Moses
    B. The Ark of the Covenant
    C. The prophet Samuel
    D. Thousands of animals to be sacrificed to God

17. How does Absalom flaunt his brief overthrow of David's throne?
    A. By destroying David's palace
    B. By killing the priests of Israel
    C. By taunting David and his army as they flee Jerusalem
    D. By sleeping with David's concubines in public

18. What event triggers the division of Israel into two kingdoms?
    A. Jeroboam desecrates the Temple in Jerusalem.
    B. Jeroboam leads a rebellion against the wicked King Rehoboam.
    C. King Solomon's sons fight over the throne.
    D. Rehoboam wants the tribe of Judah to secede from the twelve tribes.

19. Who is Elisha?
    A. Elijah
    B. Elijah's opponent
    C. Elijah's apprentice and successor
    D. Elijah's son

20. What do the deaths of King Ahab and his wife Jezebel have in common?
    A. Elijah stabs them in their sleep.
    B. Dogs eat the blood of their dead bodies.
    C. The Philistines gouge out their eyes.
    D. They die cursing God.

21. Which Jewish festival results from the events in Esther?
    A. Passover
    B. Hanukkah
    C. Purim
    D. Rosh Hashanah

22. Which of the following is not one of Israel's judges?
    A. Deborah
    B. Gideon
    C. Ahab
    D. Jephthah

23. What does King Solomon do in Israel?
    A. He introduces animal sacrifices.
    B. He bans the cult of Baal worship in Israel.
    C. He builds a grand temple in Jerusalem.
    D. He forms a legendary round table of leaders and priests.

24. What is one of the main criteria in Leviticus for living in the Israelite camp?
    A. To be ceremonially clean
    B. To remain sexually abstinent
    C. To be a religious priest
    D. Not to shave

25. Why does God reprimand Job?
    A. Because Job listens to his wife and curses God
    B. Because Job does not delight in his suffering
    C. Because Job uses human knowledge to question God's ways
    D. Because Job heeds the advice of his friends

ANSWER KEY

1: D; 2: C; 3: B; 4: D; 5: D; 6: A; 7: D; 8: B; 9: B; 10: D; 11: A; 12: A; 13: B; 14: C; 15: C; 16: B; 17: D; 18: B; 19: C; 20: B; 21: C; 22: C; 23: C; 24: A; 25: C

FURTHER READING

ALTER, ROBERT and FRANK KERMODE, eds. *The Literary Guide to the Bible*. Cambridge, MA: Harvard University Press, 1987.

AUERBACH, ERICH. "Odysseus' Scar." *Mimesis: The Representation of Reality in Western Literature*. Trans. Willard R. Trask. Princeton, NJ: Princeton University Press, 1953.

BARTON, JOHN and JOHN MUDDIMAN, eds. *The Oxford Bible Commentary*. New York: Oxford University Press, 2001.

FREEDMAN, DAVID NOEL, ed. *Eerdmans Dictionary of the Bible*. Grand Rapids, MI: W. B. Eerdmans Publishing Company, 2000.

JAGERSMA, HENK. *A History of Israel in the Old Testament Period*. Trans. John Bowden. Philadelphia: Fortress Press, 1983.

MILES, JACK. *God: A Biography*. New York: Vintage Books, 1995.

NOTH, MARTIN. *The History of Israel*. 2nd ed. Trans. P. R. Ackroyd. New York: Harper and Row, 1960.

THE NEW TESTAMENT

Contents — The New Testament

CONTEXT

THE NEW TESTAMENT IS THE second, shorter part of the Christian Bible. Unlike the Old Testament, which covers hundreds of years of history, the New Testament only covers several decades, and is a collection of the religious teachings and beliefs of Christianity.

The New Testament is not a single book written by one person, but, rather, a collection of twenty-seven books written in Greek by people from various places. There are many ways to interpret the New Testament. Millions of people view it as absolutely true scripture, and use its teachings as the basis of their belief systems. Some biblical scholars interpret it as a work of literature that uses beautiful poetry to describe religious myths. Others study its ethical and philosophical ideas, as its stories of the faithful attempt to instill certain values and outline an appropriate way to live.

The books of the New Testament were written in first- or second-century Palestine, a region that at the time was under the rule of the Roman Empire. Many of the stories are based on the rituals and beliefs of Judaism, as Jesus Christ and his disciples were all Jews. As a result, both Greco-Roman culture and Judaic traditions dominate the political, social, and economic scene of the New Testament. Judaism at that time was not a single tradition or set of beliefs, but contained many different divisions within itself. These divisions figure prominently in New Testament stories. The strictest Jews, the Sadducees, were the upper class of priests. They interpreted scripture literally and adhered to rituals strictly. They were opposed to oral tradition and to the concept of eternal life, since the latter is not discussed in the Hebrew Bible, or Old Testament. The Pharisees, in contrast to the Sadducees, interpreted Jewish law for laypeople and established Jewish life outside of the temple. They were more liberal in their acceptance of scripture, regarding oral tradition and the words of prophets as scriptural as well.

Judaism at the time of Christ involved a rigid social hierarchy. The temple and the high priests who worked there were considered to be pure, holy, and closer to God than anyone else. The hierarchy continued with people who were Jews by birth, followed by converts to Judaism. Gentiles, or non-Jews, were considered by Jews to be ritually impure and not in the service of God. The New Testament documents a shift in this hierarchy. Christians challenged the system in which birth into the Israelite community determined a person's level of purity. They said, instead, that repentance and acceptance of the teachings of Jesus Christ determined a person's purity.

The writers of the books that now comprise the New Testament did not intend for their writings to replace or rival the Old Testament. The Christian scriptures were originally intended to be utilitarian documents, responding to specific needs of the early church. It was only with the passage of more than a hundred years after Jesus's death that Christians began to use the term "New Testament" to refer to the scriptures that the fledgling church was beginning to view as a single sacred unit. Early Christians viewed the New Testament as the fulfillment of promises made in the Old Testament, rather than as the replacement of the Jewish scriptures.

The historical context of the New Testament greatly influences the way we interpret it as literature. Many of the speakers in the Bible address issues and problems unique to their moment in history, and a knowledge of the various cultural forces of biblical times provides a basis for understanding the characters' motivations and reactions. Furthermore, the New Testament's role as influential religious doctrine is another context. Just as historical situations shaped the development of the New Testament, the New Testament has also influenced the progress of history. Reading religious documents as literature requires an unusual understanding of the events surrounding the writing of the text.

STRUCTURE AND COMPOSITION

Only in the second century A.D. did Christians begin to use the term "New Testament" to refer to their collection of scriptures. The New Testament as we now know it is comprised of twenty-seven books, but it was not originally written as a coherent whole. Jesus himself did not produce any written record of his work. The books that comprise the New Testament were mostly written in the century following his death, in response to specific needs of the early church and its leaders. At the time of Jesus's crucifixion in approximately 30 A.D., most of the first generation of Christians believed that the end of the world was imminent. They therefore considered it unnecessary to compose records of Jesus's life. By the mid-60s A.D., however, most Christians who had known Jesus and witnessed his actions firsthand were dying. It became necessary, then, to produce works that would testify to Jesus's life. As it became clear that the second coming of Jesus would be delayed, the leaders of the church began to compose works that would enable the nascent Christian Church to survive.

The books that comprise the New Testament can be separated into three broad categories. First are the four Gospels: Matthew, Mark, Luke, and John. "Gospel" literally means "good news." The "good news" to which these gospels refer is the life, teachings, crucifixion, and resurrection of Jesus of Nazareth. The Gospels usually appear first among the texts of the New Testament, with Matthew placed first of all. But the order of the New Testament is based on importance, not chronology. The Gospels were probably written between 65 and 110 A.D., with Mark written first and John last.

The second category of texts in the New Testament are the letters from Paul. Paul of Tarsus was an early church leader and energetic missionary who spread the Gospel of Jesus across the Roman Empire, preaching to Gentiles as well as to Jews, who were the earliest targets of missionary activity. Paul wrote many letters to various Christian communities throughout the Mediterranean, settling points of doctrine and instructing new Christians in matters of faith. By the end of the second century A.D., Christian communities had collected thirteen letters that they attributed to Paul, and each letter became known by the name of the community or individual to whom it was addressed: Romans, 1 and 2 Corinthians, Galatians, Ephesians, Philippians, Colossians, 1 and 2 Thessalonians, 1 and 2 Timothy, Titus, and Philemon. A fourteenth letter, Hebrews, long accepted by Eastern churches, was accepted by Western churches in the fourth century A.D. The actual authorship and date of composition of many of these letters is seriously disputed, but it is generally agreed that Paul wrote some of them in the 50s A:D., making them the oldest existing Christian texts.

Other books in the New Testament are somewhat harder to classify. Acts of the Apostles (known simply as Acts) is a continuation of the Gospel According to Luke, giving the history of the church in the years after Jesus's crucifixion. Acts traces the expansion of the church, as it moves out from Jerusalem and spreads throughout the Gentile world. The protagonists of the book are Peter, the chief of the Twelve Apostles, who were Jesus's closest disciples, and Paul of Tarsus, the greatest early Christian missionary. Also included in the New Testament are seven letters, known as the Letters to all Christians, or the Catholic—in its literal sense, meaning "universal"—Letters, which resemble extended homilies. These letters are generally understood to have been written after the Pauline letters: James, 1 and 2 Peter, 1, 2 and 3 John, and Jude. Finally, the Book of Revelation, written in the closing years of the first century, is an extended vision predicting the events of the end of the world and the second coming of Jesus.

In its early centuries, the church was highly decentralized. Each individual church community collected its own sacred documents. The fragmented nature of the church was complicated by the difference in intellectual tradition between the East, which spoke Greek as its scholarly language and was ruled from Byzantium following the division of the Roman Empire, and the West, which spoke Latin and was centered in Rome. The process by which individual church communities came together to decide on a canon of sacred works, and the process by which they preserved those works, is not entirely clear. Criteria that seem to have been important in canonization include the authorship of the texts—texts presumed to have been written by apostles, such as Matthew, or by those who witnessed Jesus's revelation firsthand, such as Paul, were given priority—and the importance and wide acceptance of the doctrine expressed in the texts. It is known that in the decades just before and after 200 A.D., church leaders widely accepted the sacred nature of a collection of twenty works, including the four Gospels, thirteen Pauline letters, Acts, 1 Peter, and 1 John. The remaining seven works—Hebrews, Revelation, James, 2 and 3 John, Jude, and 2 Peter—were cited from the second to the fourth centuries and accepted as scripture in some, but not all, churches. Finally, by the late fourth century, there was wide, but not absolute, agreement in the Greek East and the Latin West on a canon of twenty-seven works.

It is generally agreed that the books of the New Testament were originally written in Greek, the scholarly language current at the time, and divided into chapters and verses. It is possible that a few books of the New Testament were originally written in Aramaic, a dialect popular among the Jews of Palestine, and most likely the language that Jesus himself spoke.

PLOT OVERVIEW

PLOT OVERVIEW

THE NEW TESTAMENT IS A COLLECTION of twenty-seven books centered on the figure of Jesus of Nazareth. Each of these books has its own author, context, theme, and persuasive purpose. Combined, they comprise one of history's most abundant, diverse, complex, and fascinating texts. The books of the New Testament are traditionally divided into three categories: the Gospels, the Epistles, and the Book of Revelation.

THE GOSPELS AND ACTS OF THE APOSTLES

The Gospels of Matthew, Mark, and Luke are known as the synoptic—meaning "at one look"—Gospels because each one tells a similar story, differing only in some additions, special emphases, and particular omissions according to the interests of the author and the message the text is trying to convey. Each of the synoptic Gospels tells the story of Jesus of Nazareth, including his ministry, gathering of disciples, trial, crucifixion, and, in the case of Matthew and Luke, his resurrection. John is also a Gospel, though it is not placed with the synoptic Gospels because his story is so different. Rather than recording many of the facts about Jesus's life, the Gospel according to John focuses on the mystery and identity of Jesus as the Son of God.

Acts of the Apostles follows John, although it was intended to be the second volume of a single unit beginning with Luke. The same author wrote Luke and Acts consecutively, and while Luke is a Gospel about Jesus, Acts picks up the story at the resurrection, when the early disciples are commissioned to witness to the world. Acts is a chronological history of the first church of Christ.

THE EPISTLES

The twenty-one books following Acts are epistles, or letters, written from church leaders to churches in various parts of the world. The first fourteen of these letters are called the "Epistles of Paul" and are letters that tradition has accorded to St. Paul in his correspondence with the earliest churches in the first and second century. Historians are fairly certain that Paul himself, Christianity's first theologian and successful missionary, indisputably composed seven of the letters, and possibly could have written seven others.

The seven letters following the Epistles of Paul are called the Catholic Epistles, because they are addressed to the church as a whole rather than to particular church communities. These letters identify as their authors original apostles, biological brothers of Jesus, and John the Evangelist, although it is thought that they were actually written by students or followers of these early church luminaries. The first of the Catholic Epistles is the Letter of James, attributed to James, the brother of Jesus and leader of the Christian church in Jerusalem. Next are the First and Second Letters of Peter, which identify themselves as letters from the apostle Peter. The First, Second, and Third Letters of John attribute their authorship to John the Evangelist, and the Letter of Jude attributes itself to Jude, the brother of James, who is elsewhere identified as one of Jesus's brothers.

THE REVELATION TO JOHN

The last book in the New Testament is the Revelation to John, or Book of Revelation, the New Testament's only piece of literature in the apocalyptic genre. It describes a vision by a leader of a church community in Asia Minor living under the persecution of the Roman Empire.

CHARACTER LIST

Jesus of Nazareth The central figure of the New Testament, whose life, death, and resurrection are chronicled in the books. The four Gospels describe Jesus's life until his resurrection, and the remainder of the New Testament concerns itself with the community of followers of Jesus that steadily grows after his death.

Paul of Tarsus More than half of the books in the New Testament have been attributed to Paul of Tarsus, the great missionary who directs the spread of Christianity after the death of Jesus. In these books, Paul uses his keen mind and robust intellect to develop Christianity's first sophisticated theology. In the period immediately following Jesus's death, he is an active persecutor of Jesus's followers, but he later converts and becomes the most active proponent of Christ's disciples.

Peter The first of Jesus's disciples. Extremely devoted to Jesus and his mission, Simon is able to recognize Jesus as the Messiah before the other apostles. As a result, Jesus makes him the "rock"—renaming Simon "Peter," which means rock—on which his church would be built (Matthew 16:13–20). Although Peter denies his association with Jesus after Jesus's arrest, Peter later becomes one of the leaders of the church in Jerusalem.

John the Baptist	The forerunner to Jesus, spreading the word of Jesus's imminent arrival. John the Baptist is an old ascetic who lives in the desert, wears a loincloth, and feeds on locusts and honey.
Mary Magdalene	A female follower of Jesus since the time of his Galilean ministry, when he exorcises her of seven demons (Luke 8:2). Mary Magdalene is a close friend of Jesus. She is one of the women who discover that Jesus's body is not in his grave. Following this event, she witnesses the resurrected Jesus. She is also known as Mary of Magdala.
Pontius Pilate	As prefect, Pontius Pilate governs Judea by the authority of the Roman Empire during the time of Jesus's trial in Jerusalem. The Gospels differ on the extent of Pilate's responsibility for Jesus's crucifixion. What is clear, however, is that Pilate holds the ultimate authority to determine whether or not Jesus should be executed.
Barnabas	Praised early in Acts for his generosity toward the church, Barnabas later becomes one of Paul's traveling companions and fellow missionaries, joining Paul in spreading the Gospel among the Gentiles.
Judas Iscariot	One of the Twelve Apostles, Judas betrays Jesus to the authorities in exchange for thirty pieces of silver. According to Matthew, Judas commits suicide out of remorse (Matthew 27:3–10).

Stephen	A leader of the Hellenists, a faction of the Jewish Christians, in Jerusalem during the years after Jesus's ascension. Stephen preaches against the temple (Acts 6–7). When brought for trial before the Jewish court, Stephen seals his fate by issuing a ringing condemnation of the Jewish leadership.
Timothy	The traveling companion and fellow missionary of Paul. Timothy coauthors letters with Paul—such as 1 Corinthians and Philippians—and serves as his emissary throughout the Christian communities of the Mediterranean.
Mary, Mother of Jesus	Luke's narrative of Jesus's infancy focuses heavily on the courage and faith of Mary, who becomes impregnated by the Holy Spirit. She is also one of the only people who remains with Jesus through the crucifixion. Gospel writers who have a high esteem for the female leaders in the early church community point to Mary as a model of discipleship.
Joseph	Mary's husband. Joseph is a direct paternal descendent of the great King David, which makes Jesus an heir to the Davidic line. This heritage reinforces Jesus's place in the Jewish tradition.
Luke	A traveling companion of Paul. Christian tradition dating back to the second century A.D. claims that Luke is the author of the Gospel that bears his name and of Acts of the Apostles.

Caiaphas   The high priest who presides over Jesus's trial. Though it is Pilate who declares the verdict of Jesus's guilt, the Gospel writers are insistent that Caiaphas is also responsible for the crucifixion.

Herod the Great   The King of Palestine from 37 to 4 B.C. According to Matthew, Herod hears of Jesus's birth and decides to kill the child, who is prophesied to become king of the Jews. To evade Herod's orders, Joseph takes Jesus and Mary to Egypt.

Analysis of Major Characters

Jesus

Jesus's identity is complex and changing throughout the Gospels of the New Testament. Jesus is at once a "bright morning star" (Rev. 22:16) and a small child who worries his mother sick because he stays at the temple for three extra days (Luke 2:46). Jesus is called a "glutton and a drunkard" by those who dislike him (Matthew 11:19), and he breaks social boundaries by associating with women and the poor. Jesus tells a man seeking eternal life to "go, sell what you own, and give the money to the poor, and you will have treasure in heaven; then come, follow me" (Mark 10:21). While Jesus blesses the peace-makers, the meek, and the pure in heart, he overturns the tables of the money changers in the temple, yelling that they have made God's house "a den of robbers" (Mark 11:17). He is simultaneously a "Savior" (Luke 2:11) and a servant who lowers himself to the ground, washing the feet of his disciples (John 13:5). Jesus is bread (John 6:35), light (John 9:1), and water (John 7:38-39). He is also King of Kings, Lord of Lords (Rev. 19:16), and tells a disciple, "[J]ust as you did it to one of the least of these . . . you did it to me" (Matthew 25:40).

Peter

Simon Peter is one of the most sympathetic characters in the entire New Testament. Peter is determined to be Jesus's best disciple, but prematurely thinks he understands what it means to follow Jesus. Peter does not believe Jesus's prediction that he will deny having known Jesus, but Peter's eagerness is immature, and he does end up denying his friendship to Jesus during the terrifying series of events surrounding the trial and crucifixion. Peter realizes his mistake and weeps bitterly. He is forgiven, and remains the rock upon which Jesus says he will build his church. Peter is a model of faithful discipleship. To this day, the Catholic Church claims apostolic succession from this very Peter, whose faith was as solid as a rock, but who was also at times overeager, afraid, and all too human.

PAUL

Paul, an extremely well-educated Jew, is living in Palestine when he receives a vision of Jesus and becomes a follower. Paul, however, continues to call himself the "Jew of Jews." Christianity is indebted to Paul's tireless toil for the Gospel in the first century, and to his robust intellectual prowess, which brings Christianity from a small handful of fringe-society disciples to a church with a sophisticated theology treating such complex issues as the relationship between faith and works, and the balance between unity and diversity. It is clear that Paul, whom some have called "history's first egalitarian," develops an enormous range of church leaders, including many women, in his household churches that peppered the hillsides of the Roman Empire and the coast of the Mediterranean Sea.

Themes, Motifs, and Symbols

Themes

The New Testament's Relation to the Old Testament

Each of the books of the New Testament has a unique relationship to the Old Testament and to Judaism as a whole, ranging from the very Jewish Gospel of Matthew to the Gospel of Luke, which makes little or no reference to the Jewish scriptures. This range is largely due to the location and audience of the different authors of the New Testament. Matthew's Gospel was written for a largely Jewish group to convince them that Jesus was the hoped-for Messiah, and so he interprets Jesus as someone who relives the experience of Israel. For Matthew, everything about Jesus is prophesied in the Old Testament. The Old Testament narratives to which Matthew refers served as ways in which early followers of Jesus could make sense out of his birth, death, and resurrection. In contrast, Luke makes little or no reference to the Hebrew scriptures because they would have been unfamiliar to his largely Gentile audience.

Paul introduces yet another perspective on the Hebrew Scriptures with his theology of "faith versus works," which states that through Christ we are saved "through grace alone," not through doing good works. Paul contrasts Christianity's emphasis on the grace of God and the faith of the believer with the Jewish insistence on the law as the necessary means for salvation. Paul's theology inaugurates a strong anti-Jewish tradition in Christianity, which claims that Christianity is a higher, more spiritual tradition than Judaism. This claim is called Christian supercessionism because it is based on the idea that the New Testament supercedes the Old Testament. Supercessionists believe that the laws laid down in the Old Testament are external, in the sense that they regulate human behaviors rather than spiritual states, and that these laws become unnecessary through Christ. Supercessionism simplifies the rich and subtle theology of the Old Testament, which makes no such distinction between faith and works.

SALVATION FOR SOCIAL OUTCASTS

Some scholars have argued that the New Testament's references to sinners actually referred to those who were marginalized, poor, cast out, orphaned, diseased, or widowed. Jesus not only promises salvation to such sinners, but goes so far as to call their poverty itself "blessed" throughout the Gospels. At many points in Jesus's ministry, he shocks mainstream Jews by associating with, ministering to, and healing people who are cast out, poor, and sick. Some have argued that a prominent theme in the Gospels is Jesus's good news to such people and an invitation to the rich to join them.

SALVATION THROUGH FAITH IN CHRIST

In his final letter to the new churches in Romans, Paul summarizes his lifelong question about the relationship between Jewish law, which requires certain observances and actions, and faith in the grace offered by God through Jesus Christ, which is given freely and without regard for good works. This issue was particularly problematic in Rome because the early church consisted both of Jewish followers of Christ, who observed the law, and Gentile followers, to whom the law was relatively unknown. Paul concludes that the law is a gift from God, and can help people become more faithful, but ultimately we are justified by faith alone, and the grace of God is available to both Jews and Gentiles. In the end, Paul declares that only minimal observance of Jewish law is necessary to be a follower of Jesus—who himself, interestingly enough, was a law-abiding Jew.

MOTIFS

GEOGRAPHY

The Gospel of Mark takes us on a vivid journey through the roads of first-century Palestine, from the small Galilean villages to Jerusalem, where Jesus's trial and crucifixion take place. The shifts from location to location in the narrative are often abrupt and hasty, but these movements serve an important purpose in that they teach believers that Christian discipleship means following in the footsteps of Jesus. Believers are to follow his progress in their imaginations, as one follows a character in a story, sympathizing with him in his progression to the cross. Jesus's trail toward the cross offers a warning to potential followers that discipleship may involve persecution and suffering, and will call for unremitting faithfulness on the part of the disciple.

SYMBOLS

THE KINGDOM OF HEAVEN

The longest section of Matthew's Gospel is his "proclamation" (Matthew 4:17–16:20), in which he issues a number of declarations about the kingdom of heaven. Matthew likens God's kingdom to a small mustard seed, which has in it the potential to grow into a "tree so that the birds of the air come and make nests in its branches," something startlingly different in size and appearance from its humble beginnings. Matthew's proclamations about the kingdom of God symbolize the tantalizing fruits yielded by a life lived in obedience to the commandments of Christ. His use of the phrase "kingdom of heaven" also discloses Matthew's Jewish roots, as in Jewish custom one could not utter God's name.

THE GOOD SAMARITAN

In one of the New Testament's most well known parables, Luke tells us that Jesus used this story as the answer to a man's question, "Who is my neighbor?" Jesus describes a man lying on the road, dying. Neither a passing priest nor a Levite helps him, because touching a dead body was considered utterly impure. The Samaritan, however, rescues the man, thereby breaking two social conventions—associating with what could be a corpse, and crossing the border between the rival communities of Jews and Samaritans. The Samaritan can be understood to symbolize both Christ's message that the poor and outcast are blessed, and that Christ's message is for Gentiles as well as Jews.

WATER, BREAD, LIGHT

In John's Gospel, Jesus is symbolized by the life-giving matter of everyday existence: water, bread, light, and words. Water and bread, in particular, are used repeatedly. While speaking with a Samaritan woman at the well, Jesus tells her, "water that I will give will become in them a spring of water gushing up to eternal life." She says in reply, "[S]ir, give me this water so that I may never be thirsty or have to keep coming here to draw water." John uses this symbol of water to illustrate that Jesus's gift is abundant and life-giving.

THE OLIVE TREE

In Romans 11:17–24, the olive tree symbolizes the salvation of the Gentiles and of Israel. The tree, including the root and branches, is Israel. The branches broken off are the Jews who do not believe in Jesus Christ, while the branches grafted on are Gentiles who believe in Christ. Having been made part of the tree only because of faith—rather than birth, obedience to the law, or works—the

Gentile believers have no reason for pride, since the God who has grafted them on has the power to cut them off.

The Body

In 1 Corinthians 12:12, Paul writes about the variety of spiritual gifts that exist using the image of the human body to convey that each of these different gifts is needed, just as every part of the body is needed. The church is Christ's body. Paul writes, "For just as the body is one and has many members, all the members of the body, though many, are one body, so it is with Christ. For in the one Spirit we were all baptized into one body—Jews or Greeks, slaves or free—and we were all made to drink of one Spirit." Paul uses this symbol as a way to deal with the difficult issue of balancing unity and diversity in his early churches, saying that though we are all uniquely gifted individuals, we are also all parts of the one united body of Christ.

Summary and Analysis

The Gospel According to Matthew (Matthew)

> [T]he Son of man came eating and drinking, and
> they say, "Look, a glutton and a drunkard, a
> friend of tax collectors and sinners!" Yet wisdom
> is vindicated by her deeds.
>
> *(See* QUOTATIONS, *p. 204)*

INTRODUCTION

In the second century A.D., the Gospel of Matthew was placed at
the very beginning of the New Testament. It was believed to be
the first Gospel written, though we now know that the Gospel
of Mark dates earlier. Because it is the Gospel most intensely
concerned with issues related to Judaism, it provides an appropriate
transition from the Old Testament to the New Testament in the
Christian Bible. Matthew became the most important of all Gospel
texts for first- and second-century Christians because it contains
all the elements important to the early church: the story about
Jesus's miraculous conception; an explanation of the importance
of liturgy, law, discipleship, and teaching; and an account of Jesus's
life and death. The Gospel of Matthew has long been considered
the most important of the four Gospels.

Though second-century church tradition holds that the
author of the Gospel is Matthew, a former tax collector and one
of Jesus's Twelve Apostles, also known as Levi, scholars today
maintain that we have no direct evidence of Matthew's authorship.
Because the Gospel of Matthew relies heavily on the earlier Gospel

of Mark, as well as late first-century oral tradition for its description of events in Christ's life, it is unlikely that the author of the Gospel of Matthew was an eyewitness to the life of Christ. Instead, the author was probably a Jewish member of a learned community in which study and teaching were passionate forms of piety, and the Gospel was probably written between 80 and 90 A.D.

Matthew is arranged in seven parts. An introductory segment gives the story of Jesus's miraculous birth and the origin of his ministry, and a conclusion gives the story of the Last Supper, Jesus's trial and crucifixion, and the resurrection. In the middle are five structurally parallel sections. In each section, a narrative segment—interrupted occasionally by dialogue and brief homilies—tells of Jesus's miracles and actions. Closing each section, Jesus preaches a long sermon that responds to the lessons learned in the narrative section. The Sermon on the Mount, which introduces the basic elements of the Christian message, follows Jesus's first venture into ministry (5:1–7:29). The Mission Sermon, which empowers Jesus's apostles, follows Jesus's recognition that more teachers and preachers are necessary (10:1–42). The mysterious Sermon in Parables responds to Jesus's frustration with the fact that many people do not understand or accept his message (13:1–52). The Sermon on the Church responds to the need to establisha lasting fraternity of Christians (18:1–35). Finally, the Eschatological Sermon, which addresses the end of the world, responds to the developing certainty that Jesus will be crucified (23:1–25:46).

SUMMARY

Matthew traces Jesus's ancestors back to the biblical patriarch Abraham, the founding father of the Israelite people. Matthew describes Jesus's conception, when his mother, Mary, was "found to be with child from the Holy Spirit" (1:18). Matthew focuses very little on Mary herself, and praises Joseph for not abandoning his fiancée.

Jesus is born in Bethlehem, where he and his parents are visited by wise men from the East bearing gifts. The wise men follow a star to Bethlehem. Their king, Herod the Great, hears the rumor that a baby named Jesus is the "king of the Jews" (2:2). Herod orders all young children in Bethlehem to be killed. To escape the king's wrath, Joseph, Mary, and Jesus flee to Egypt. Joseph and his family return to Israel after Herod's death, but then move to Nazareth, a town in the northern district known as Galilee.

Years pass, and Jesus grows up. A man in a loincloth, who lives by eating wild honey and locusts, begins to prophesy throughout Judea, foretelling of Jesus as the one who will come to "baptize you with the Holy Spirit and fire" (3:11). This prophet, John the Baptist, who is likely a member of the ascetic Jewish Essene community, eventually meets Jesus. John baptizes Jesus, and Jesus receives the blessing of God, who says, "This is my Son, the Beloved" (3:17). Jesus is led into the wilderness for forty days without food or water to be tested by Satan. Jesus emerges unscathed and triumphant, and begins to preach his central, most often repeated proclamation: "Repent! For the kingdom of heaven has come near" (4:17). His ministry begins.

Matthew mentions Jesus's earliest followers: Simon Peter, Andrew, James, and John. Once Jesus accumulates this small group of Jewish followers, he begins to preach. His early ministry reaches a peak when he gives a sermon famously known as the Sermon on the Mount, which deeply impresses his increasingly large group of followers (5:1–7:29). The sermon emphasizes humility, obedience, love of one's neighbor, the proper method of prayer, and trust in God. Jesus says that the poor, meek, and hungry are blessed.

As he travels through Galilee, Jesus continues to attract crowds. Matthew relates ten of Jesus's miracles, which are also described in the Gospel of Mark. Jesus cures a leper, a paralytic, a hemorrhaging woman, a centurion's servant, and Peter's mother-in-law. He also calms a storm, exorcizes demons, gives eyesight to the blind, and brings a dead girl back to life. Jesus resolves to "send out laborers" to minister to the Gentiles, to whom he refers as lost sheep (9:38). Jesus appoints twelve disciples, telling them that they will be persecuted but they should not be afraid. Jesus instructs the apostles to preach that the "kingdom of heaven has come near," and to heal the sick, raise the dead, cleanse lepers, and cast out demons, all without payment (10:7).

In Chapter 11, Matthew interrupts his account of Jesus and his disciples' mission to focus on Jesus himself. He gives an account of the opposition Jesus faces. Some people disapprove of his association with sinners, tax collectors, and prostitutes. They call him a glutton and a drunkard. In the face of such rejection, Jesus does not apologize, but, rather, admonishes those who reject him.

Jesus responds to his challengers with a collection of parables. Matthew describes several of the parables—the parables of the sower, the weeds, the mustard seed, and the leaven—that Jesus tells to the crowds that gather to listen to him (13:1–33). Jesus then explains that his disciples are part of his family.

Jesus's ministry of healing, cleansing, and raising the dead continues as he travels throughout Galilee. But he is rejected in his hometown of Nazareth, where his friends and neighbors deride him. He continues to perform miracles, but the people become increasingly resistant and disbelieving. Jesus multiplies loaves and fish, feeding thousands on very little food. He heals the sick and continues to preach the message of spiritual righteousness. Yet Jesus repeatedly finds that his disciples still lack faith in him. When he miraculously walks across the water to them, they assume he must be a ghost. Even after he multiplies the loaves, they fear hunger. Only Simon properly professes his faith, "You are the Messiah, the Son of the living God" (16:16). Jesus renames Simon "Peter," a name whose Greek form is identical to the Greek word "rock." Jesus announces, "You are Peter, and on this rock I will build my church" (16:18). Jesus then lays out the rules for communal relations among Christians, emphasizing forgiveness, humility, and obedience to his teachings.

Jesus continues to preach. He forbids divorce and advocates chastity, while expounding the virtues of asceticism. He warns against the pitfalls of wealth, teaches forgiveness, and welcomes children. In Jerusalem, cheering crowds await him. People "spread their cloaks on the road, and others cut branches from the trees and spread them on the road" (21:8). Upon his arrival in Jerusalem, Jesus expels money changers from the Jewish temple and defies the chief priests and elders, saying, "My house shall be called a house of prayer, but you are making it a den of robbers" (21:13). Jesus's action earns him the support of the crowds. He chastises Jewish leaders, telling them they have been poor caretakers of the temple and that the people have been hypocritical, focusing on technical legal issues rather than "justice and mercy and faith" (23:23). Seeing the wickedness of Jerusalem, and foreseeing God's punishment of the wicked, Jesus warns his disciples to be prepared for the end of the world. He says that tribulations will precede the final judgment, but that the Son of man—Jesus himself—will come, and that the righteous will be saved.

In Chapter 26, Jesus celebrates the Last Supper with the disciples. Jesus indicates that Judas, one of his disciples, will betray him. Jesus predicts that after his death, the other disciples will flee, and Peter will also betray him. When he breaks bread and drinks wine with the disciples, Jesus initiates a ritual that later becomes known as the Eucharist, the consumption of bread and wine symbolizing Jesus's body and blood. After dining with the apostles, Jesus goes into a garden called Gethsemane. There he prays, asking God if it is possible to escape the impending suffering. As Jesus is leaving the garden, Judas approaches, accompanied by a mob and a great number of Roman soldiers. Judas kisses Jesus in order to show the angry mob which man claims to be the Son of God.

Jesus is arrested and brought before the Jewish court, where he is convicted of blasphemy. Caiaphas, the high priest, sends him to Pontius Pilate, the governor of Rome, for a final verdict. Pilate looks surprisingly weak and undecided. He turns to the crowd for the judgment and they all chant, "Let him be crucified!" (27:22). Pilate concedes. Jesus is led out, crowned with thorns, mocked, and crucified. On the cross, Jesus cries out, "My God, my God, why have you forsaken me?" and then dies (27:46). Matthew notes the presence of "many women" at the execution, including "Mary Magdalene, and Mary the mother of James and Joseph, and the mother of the sons of Zebedee" (27:56). Jesus is buried by Joseph of Arimathea and a guard is set over the tomb. On the first day of the week, three days after the crucifixion, Mary Magdalene and Mary go to visit Jesus's tomb in order to anoint his body with oils and spices according to Jewish custom, but they find the tomb empty. Astonished, they see an angel who tells them that Jesus has been resurrected from the dead and that he can be found in Galilee. The women leave the tomb both happy and afraid. Suddenly, Jesus greets them and asks them to tell his disciples to meet him in Galilee. After the women leave, the guards tell the city's chief priests what has happened, and the priests bribe the guards to report that Jesus's body was stolen while they were sleeping. In Galilee, Jesus commissions his disciples to teach and baptize non-believers as they travel throughout the world.

ANALYSIS

The Gospel of Matthew is strongly connected to the Old Testament. Although Matthew, Mark, Luke, and John all cite Old Testament prophesies that they regard as having been fulfilled in the person and works of Jesus, Matthew is particularly careful to point out that Jesus's teachings are compatible with Judaism, and to insist that Jesus's life fulfills Old Testament prophesies. Matthew portrays Jesus as a second, greater Moses, an important prophet in the Old Testament. Just as Moses gave his law from Mount Sinai in the Old Testament, Jesus preaches his new laws in a sermon he gives from a mountain. Like Moses, the young Jesus hides in Egypt from the wrath of a vengeful king. Finally, Jesus is tempted for forty days and forty nights in the wilderness, while Moses and his people wandered the wilderness for forty years.

Matthew further emphasizes Jesus's ties to Jewish tradition by tracing Jesus's ancestry to Abraham, the father of the Jewish people. Matthew clearly speaks from within the Jewish tradition to a largely Jewish audience. But at the same time, Matthew's Gospel contains some of the most vehement anti-Jewish polemic in the entire New Testament. For example, Matthew challenges mere external obedience to religious law, valuing instead an internal spiritual transformation: "You have heard that it was said 'You shall love your neighbor and hate your enemy.' But I say to you, Love your enemies and pray for those who persecute you" (5:43). It is also possible to interpret such passages as Jesus's reinterpretation of Jewish law rather than his rejection of it. Jesus is simply reminding his community what Jewish law already indicates: that God demands absolute obedience and not just the appearance of obedience.

Matthew is the most carefully structured of the Gospels: it proceeds through an introduction; five central segments, each designed with a concluding sermon that responds to the concerns raised in the preceding narrative; and a conclusion detailing Jesus's Passion. Matthew's careful construction reflects his Gospel's concern with rhetorical structure. In contrast with Mark's spare style and Luke's formal tone, Matthew's rhetoric is meant to be stirring. Many readers regard the five sermons in which Matthew conveys Jesus's teachings as some of the finest prose in the New Testament. The Sermon on the Mount is Matthew's greatest composition, in which he reveals his talent for epigrams, balanced sentences, and rhetorical shifts as he moves the sermon from its graceful and quietly powerful opening, "Blessed are the poor in spirit, for theirs is the kingdom of heaven" (5:3), to its tempestuous finale, "The rain fell, and the floods came, and the winds blew and beat against that house, and it fell—and great was its fall!" (7:27).

THE GOSPEL ACCORDING TO MARK (MARK)

INTRODUCTION

For a long time, the Gospel of Mark was the least popular of the Gospels, both among scholars and general readers. Mark's literary style is somewhat dull—for example, he begins a great number of sentences with the word "then." Luke and Matthew both contain the same story of Jesus's life, but in more sophisticated prose. Mark also leaves out accounts of Jesus's birth, the Sermon on the Mount, and several of the most well known parables. Mark became more popular, however, when biblical scholars discovered it was the earliest written of the four Gospels, and was probably the primary source of information for the writers of Luke and Matthew. Moreover, because neither Jesus nor his original disciples left any writings behind, the Gospel of Mark is the closest document to an original source on Jesus's life that currently exists. The presumed author of the Gospel of Mark, John Mark, was familiar with Peter, Jesus's closest disciple. Indeed, Mark is the New Testament historian who comes closest to witnessing the actual life of Jesus. Though Mark's Gospel certainly comes to us through his own personal lens, scholars are fairly confident that Mark is a reliable source of information for understanding Jesus's life, ministry, and crucifixion. As a result of its proximity to original sources, the Gospel of Mark has transformed from a book disregarded for its lowly prose to one of the most important books in the New Testament. Its historical importance has affected its evaluation by literary scholars as well. Though crude and terse, the Gospel of Mark is vivid and concrete. Action dominates. A dramatic sense of urgency is present, and Mark has a developed sense of irony that permeates the Gospel.

SUMMARY

The Gospel According to Mark has no story of Jesus's birth. Instead, Mark's story begins by describing Jesus's adult life, introducing it with the words, "The beginning of the good news of Jesus Christ, the Son of God" (1:1). Mark tells of John the Baptist, who predicts the coming of a man more powerful than himself. After John baptizes Jesus with water, the Holy Spirit of God recognizes Jesus as his son, saying, "You are my Son, the Beloved" (1:11). Jesus goes to the wilderness, where Satan tests him for forty days, and Jesus emerges triumphant.

Jesus travels to Galilee, the northern region of Israel. He gathers his first disciples, Simon and Andrew, two Jewish brothers who are both fishermen. Jesus asks them to follow him, saying that he will show them how to fish for people rather than for fish. Simon and Andrew, as well as James and John, drop their nets and follow him. Jesus exhibits his authority in Galilee, where he cleanses a leper (1:40–45). Mark reports that Jesus heals a paralytic, Simon's sick mother-in-law, and a man with a withered hand. The miracles cause the crowds that gather to watch Jesus to become bewildered, fearful, and antagonistic. The Pharisees and followers of Herod begin plotting to kill Jesus. Jesus stays focused on his ministry.

Jesus's ministry attracts many followers. The miracle stories become increasingly longer and more elaborate, emphasizing the supernatural power of Jesus's authority. Mark says that "even wind and sea obey him" (4:35–41). Simultaneously, Jesus becomes increasingly misunderstood and rejected, even by his own apostles. Jesus notes his disciples' frequent misunderstandings of his message. Jesus's power continues to reveal itself in his control over nature: he calms a storm, cures a man possessed by a demon, and revives a dead young girl. Despite his successes, however, he continues to be reviled in his own hometown of Nazareth.

The story of Jesus's ministry reaches King Herod Antipas, the ruler of Galilee who beheaded John the Baptist. Jesus disperses the apostles, charging them with the responsibility to spread the Gospel and to heal the sick. When the apostles rejoin Jesus, they are once again swarmed with people eager to hear Jesus's message. Through a miracle, Jesus divides five loaves of bread and two fish and feeds all 5,000 people. His disciples, however, seem not to understand the magnitude of his miracle: when he walks on water, they are shocked. The Pharisees, who are upset at Jesus's abandonment of the traditional Jewish laws, question Jesus. He responds by pointing out that it is important to obey the spirit of the law rather than simply going through the technical actions that the law proscribes. Jesus preaches that human intention, not behavior, determines righteousness.

Jesus travels again through northern Palestine. He heals a deaf man and the child of a Gentile, and works a second miracle in which he multiplies a small amount of bread and fish to feed 4,000 people. His disciples, however, continue to misunderstand the significance of his actions. Peter, the foremost of the disciples, seems to be the only one who recognizes Jesus's divine nature. Jesus begins to foresee his own crucifixion and resurrection. He continues to travel across Galilee, but shifts his emphasis to preaching rather than working miracles. He appears to some of his disciples to be transfigured, made brilliantly white. Jesus explains that John the Baptist served as his Elijah, predicting his arrival. He preaches against divorce and remarriage. He announces that young children, in their innocence, are models for righteous behavior, and that the rich will have great difficulty entering the kingdom of God. He teaches, despite the sacrifices necessary to enter the kingdom, it will be worth it: "Many who are first will be last, and the last, first" (10:31).

Finally, Jesus journeys to Jerusalem, where he drives the money changers from the temple and begins preaching his Gospel. He is well received by the common people but hated by the priests and the scribes. However, he successfully defends himself against the priests' verbal attacks. He teaches that obedience to Caesar is important, that the dead will be resurrected, that loving one's neighbor is the greatest commandment, and that the End of Days will soon come, bringing God's retribution on the unjust and the return of the Son of man.

Eventually, Jesus allows himself to succumb to the conspiracy against him. At the Passover Seder, Jesus institutes the Christian sacrament of the Eucharist, telling his followers to eat and drink his symbolic body and blood. At the dinner, Jesus says that one of his disciples will betray him. The disciples are surprised, each asking, "Surely, not I?" (14:19). After dinner, Jesus goes to a garden called Gethsemane and prays while Peter, James, and John wait nearby. The three disciples fall asleep three times, though Jesus returns each time and asks them to stay awake with him as he prays. Jesus prays to God that, if possible, he might avoid his imminent suffering.

Jesus is leaving the garden with Peter, James, and John when Judas Iscariot, one of the apostles, arrives with the city's chief priests and a crowd carrying swords and clubs. Judas kisses Jesus, indicating to the priests Jesus's identity. The priests arrest Jesus and take him to the court of the high priest. There, Jesus publicly claims that he is "the Messiah, the Son of the Blessed One," and the Jews deliver him to Pontius Pilate, the Roman governor, who agrees to crucify him (14:61). On the cross, Jesus cries out, "My God, my God, why have you forsaken me?" (15:34). He dies and is buried by Joseph of Arimathea, a righteous Jew. When Mary Magdalene and other women come to Jesus's grave on the third day after the crucifixion, however, they find it empty. A young man tells them that Jesus has risen from the grave. Jesus then appears in resurrected form to Mary, Mary Magdalene, and the apostles.

ANALYSIS

Mark's Gospel is often disconnected, and at times difficult to read as a logically progressing narrative. This Gospel is brief and concise, reading almost like an outline, with little effort made to connect the roughly chronological list of incidents. Mark's Gospel also tends to interrupt itself by introducing information of marginal relevance. For example, Mark interrupts the story of the dispersal of the apostles and their return with the anecdote about Herod Antipas and John the Baptist. The Gospels of Matthew and Luke rely on Mark for much of their information, and they flesh out the bare-bones outline, adding additional information and employing a more fluid and elaborate style. The relationship between these first three Gospels is extremely complex. They are often approached as a group because of their strong similarities, and because of the way in which they appear to have been influenced by each other or by common sources. Because of their interconnectedness, they are called "synoptic," meaning that they can be looked at "with one glance."

The Gospel of Mark does show some evidence of tight, purposeful construction. Mark can be divided into two sections. The first, from 1:1 to 8:26, concerns itself with Jesus's ministry in Galilee, beginning with John the Baptist's prophecy proclaiming the advent of the Messiah. The second, from 8:27 to 16:20, tells the story of Jesus's prediction of his own suffering, crucifixion, and resurrection.

Mark's Gospel constantly presumes that the end of the world is imminent. Therefore, when the end of time never came, early Christian communities had difficulty interpreting passages such as the thirteenth chapter of Mark, whose apocalyptic vision is urgent, striking, and confident. Another prominent motif of Mark is secrecy. Mark writes that the kingdom is near, the time has come, but only a few are privy to any knowledge of it. This motif is known as the Messianic Secret. For example, Mark refers to secrecy in relation to the kingdom of God in 4:11-12:

> And he said to them, "To you has been given the secret of the kingdom of God, but for those outside everything comes in parables, in order that / 'they may indeed look but not perceive.'"

For Mark, Jesus's parables are riddles meant to be understood only by a select few. However, as the Gospel unfolds, the disciples do not maintain their privileged position.

As Mark tells his story, the twelve disciples persistently, even increasingly, fail to understand Jesus. Ultimately, two of them betray him, the rest abandon him, and at the end he is crucified alone until two of his bravest disciples, Mary Magdalene and Mary, return and find his tomb empty. If anyone is loyal in this Gospel, it is the Galilean women who look on Jesus's crucifixion from a distance and come to bury him. The Gospel of Mark is brutal on the disciples; some scholars suggest that Mark is trying to express his theme that when one follows Christ, one must be prepared for the experiences of misunderstanding and even persecution. Mark's model of discipleship includes the experiences of failure and doubt as part of the process of coming to understand the full meaning of Jesus. For Mark, discipleship means debating, questioning, stumbling, and learning. It involves suffering, service to others, poverty, and faithfulness despite persecution. It is strange that the Gospel of Mark ends so abruptly; scholars generally agree that the Gospel of Mark ends with verse 16:8, and that verses 16:9–20 were a later addition to the manuscript. The ending at 16:8 is confusing: Jesus's body is gone, and in his place an angel appears to Mary Magdalene and others, charging them to tell Peter of Jesus's resurrection. The women fail to fulfill this command: "So they went out and fled from the tomb, for the terror and amazement had seized them; and they said nothing to anyone, for they were afraid" (16:8). This ending is hardly triumphant, and verses 16:9–20 preserve Mark's original message. Jesus appears to his apostles, and victory seems assured: "And they went out and proclaimed the good news everywhere, while the Lord worked with them and confirmed the message by the signs that accompanied it" (16:20).

THE GOSPEL ACCORDING TO LUKE (LUKE)

INTRODUCTION

> *A sower went out to sow his seed; and as he*
> *sowed, some fell on the path, and was trampled*
> *on, and the birds of the air ate it up.*
> (See QUOTATIONS, p. 207)

The final editors of the New Testament separated the Gospel
According to Luke and Acts of the Apostles, which were originally
written by the same author in a single two-volume work. The Gospel
of Luke is the unit's first half and narrates the birth, ministry, death,
and resurrection of Jesus. The second half, which contains Acts of
the Apostles, is one of the first works to chronicle church history,
tracing events from the resurrection of Jesus to the time when the
apostle Paul is traveling and proclaiming the Gospel "with all boldness and without hindrance" (Acts 28:31). Luke's Gospel features
an introductory prologue typical of a historian in antiquity. He
writes, "I too, decided, after investigating everything carefully from
the very first, to write an orderly account for you, most excellent
Theophilus, so that you may know the truth concerning the things
about which you have been instructed" (1:3–4). Luke's orderly
account relies on eyewitnesses of Jesus and the earliest disciples,
though he could not have been an eyewitness himself. The Gospel
of Luke dates from between 75 and 85 A.D., around the same time
as Matthew. The author relies most likely on the Gospel of Mark
and other stories circulating orally during his lifetime. Luke's Greek
is the polished work of a gifted literary artist, indicating that Luke
was a cultivated, well-educated man.

SUMMARY

After his introduction, Luke lays out, in two chapters, the parallel miraculous births of Jesus of Nazareth and the man who becomes his prophet, John the Baptist. The angel Gabriel appears to Zechariah, telling him that his wife Elizabeth, formerly barren, is pregnant. Soon afterward, Gabriel appears to Elizabeth's relative, the virgin Mary, who is betrothed to Joseph, telling her that she too is going to give birth to a child by the grace of the Holy Spirit. Mary visits Elizabeth, and Elizabeth prophesies that Mary will be "the mother of my Lord" (1:43). Mary, rejoicing, utters the prayer now known as the Magnificat: "My soul magnifies the Lord" (1:46). John is born, and his father, Zechariah—who had been struck mute for the duration of the pregnancy as a punishment for his lack of belief in Gabriel's prophecy—utters a prayer, the Benedictus: "Blessed be the Lord, God of Israel . . ." (1:68). Mary and Joseph travel from their home in Nazareth to Bethlehem to partake in a census, and there, in a manger, Jesus is born. When Jesus is presented at the temple, where all firstborn males are brought, two Jewish prophets, Simeon and Anna, recognize the sanctity of the child. As yet, however, nobody realizes his true significance. When Mary finds the adolescent Jesus sitting in the temple among the sages, she does not understand his remark, "Why were you searching for me? Did you not know I must be in my Father's house?" (2:49).

Jesus grows to maturity and is baptized in the desert of Judea by John the Baptist, who has begun his advocacy of baptismal repentance for the forgiveness of sins, and prophesies the advent of Jesus. John, however, is soon imprisoned by Herod Antipas, the ruler of the northern Galilee region. After Jesus's baptism, Luke gives Jesus's genealogy, stretching back to the first man, Adam, who is said to be "son of God" (3:38). We are told of Satan unsuccessfully testing Jesus for forty days in the wilderness. Returning from the wilderness, Jesus begins his ministry. He is rejected in his hometown of Nazareth and takes to wandering throughout Galilee, where he works many miracles, including the exorcism of a demoniac and many other cures. He works a miracle enabling Simon Peter, a fisherman, to catch many fish, and thereby attracts Simon Peter, as well as James and John, the sons of Zebedee, as his first apostles. Later, these three apostles are joined by nine others. In this first stage of his ministry, Jesus also begins to encounter opposition from the Pharisees, who question his adherence to traditional Jewish laws governing Sabbath observance, fasting, and consorting with sinners. Despite this opposition, his fame grows, and he attracts a great crowd to whom he delivers a shorter version of Matthew's great Sermon on the Mount, telling his followers to "love your enemies, do good to those who hate you" (6:27).

Jesus goes to Capernaum, where he cures the servant of a Roman centurion and restores the son of a widow to life. When John the Baptist, imprisoned, sends messengers to ask Jesus who he is, Jesus responds only by pointing out the many miracles he has worked. Jesus commends John the Baptist's ministry and laments the fact that his contemporaries have refused to listen to John and to Jesus himself. Jesus's travels continue as he preaches and works miracles. Accepting the ministrations of a wicked woman, Jesus shows that he forgives even the most wretched of sinners. He explains in a parable that the seed of the word of God will only sprout in noble and generous hearts, and that the true family of Jesus is not his mother and siblings, but those who hear the word of God. Among his miracles, he calms a storm; cures a man possessed by a demon, and a woman with a hemorrhage; and revives the daughter of Jairus. Jesus sends the Twelve Apostles out to preach the Gospel and to cure illness. On their return, Jesus is swarmed by people eager to hear his preaching. He works the miracle of the loaves and fish for them, multiplying scant food to feed 5,000 people. When he questions the faith of his apostles, asking, "Who do you say that I am?", Peter replies, "The Messiah of God" (9:20). Immediately after this event, Jesus gives the first of his three prophecies of the Passion, during which he predicts that he will be executed and resurrected. A set of brief spiritual messages ensues: following Christ means a total abnegation of the self; the kingdom of God is imminent; and humility is crucial, as "the least among all of you is the greatest" (9:48).

Jesus begins to travel toward Jerusalem. His journey is punctuated by a number of brief episodes. He appoints seventy missionaries to spread his word among all the nations, reminds a lawyer that love toward God and one's neighbors is the most important virtue, and explains that all those who act kindly, regardless of whether they are Jew or Gentile, are neighbors. He tells his disciples how they should pray, teaching them the Lord's Prayer and telling them that any sincere request will be granted by God. Jesus says, "Ask, and it will be given you" (11:9). He cautions extensively against ostentation and against the accumulation of wealth. Responding to attacks from the Pharisees, he accuses them of hypocrisy, for caring more about the letter of the law than about "justice and the love of God" (11:42). Perhaps anticipating further attacks by disbelievers, he tells his followers to be bold in asserting the Gospel's truth, and to be prepared for the unexpected final judgment. He works his way toward Jerusalem, delivering parables and lessons whose morals center around faith in God: the importance of repentance; the virtues of humility and kindness; the dangers of riches; the reward of total renunciation of the worldly in favor of the divine; and the ruin that will come to those who fail to listen to God's word.

Arriving in Jerusalem, Jesus foresees the destruction of the great city as a punishment for its failure to recognize him. Driving away the merchants, Jesus begins to preach in the temple and wins the allegiance of the common people. He refuses to justify his authority to the chief priests and elders who oppose him. Chastising them, he compares them to wicked tenants, who will be evicted and punished by the Lord, the true owner of the temple. The Jewish leaders attempt to entrap Jesus verbally, but he subverts them while asserting the importance of obedience to secular authority and belief in the resurrection of the dead. Jesus prophesies that the mighty temple will be destroyed and speaks of the great torment that will accompany the Apocalypse, preceding the End of Days and the return of the Son of man, one of Christ's titles.

Passover arrives, and Jesus celebrates the traditional Seder meal with his disciples. At the Seder, he institutes the Eucharist, the ritual consumption of wine and bread as symbols of Jesus's blood and body, signs of the new covenant. Jesus cautions his disciples not to fight about who among them is greatest, and reminds them that serving is greater than being served. He promises them rewards for their faithfulness. He also foretells that Simon Peter will falter in his faith. This prophecy proves true when, soon afterward, the chief priests and elders arrest Jesus, who has been betrayed by Judas Iscariot, one of the apostles. Peter, frightened, thrice denies all knowledge of Jesus. Brought before the Sanhedrin, the Jewish court, Jesus neither affirms nor denies his identity as God's son, answering questions with the simple statement, "You say that I am" (22:70). The court considers this statement a confession and brings him before the Roman prefect, Pilate. Pilate hesitates to convict Jesus, but the chief priests and elders eventually convince Pilate to sentence Jesus to death. Jesus is crucified, going to his death with the words, "Father, forgive them; for they do not know what they are doing," and is viciously mocked by the Roman guards (23:34). Joseph of Arimathea buries him.

On Sunday, the third day after Jesus's Friday crucifixion, some female followers of Jesus, including Mary Magdalene, go to his gravesite but find him gone. Angels appear and tell them that Jesus has been resurrected from the dead. The women tell the apostles what they have seen, but the apostles do not believe them. Peter goes to check the grave himself, and is amazed at not finding Jesus's body. Finally, Jesus appears to the dumbfounded disciples and gives them his last instructions: "in his name to all nations, beginning from Jerusalem. You are witnesses of these things" (24:47–48).

ANALYSIS

Although the Gospels of Matthew, Mark, and Luke tell basically the same story, there are important differences between the Gospels that help identify the special interests of each author. A comparison of the different genealogies of Jesus offers a good example. In Matthew's Gospel, Jesus's family lineage is traced back through important Jewish families, culminating with Abraham, the father of the Jewish people. This line of descent fits well with Matthew's emphasis on Jesus's continuity with the Old Testament and the Jewish people. In contrast, Luke's genealogy downplays Judaic roots and traces Jesus's parentage to Adam, the universal man of the Old Testament. Luke's emphasis on Jesus's common humanity gives scholars reason to think that Luke could have been a learned Gentile speaking to a largely Gentile audience. Although he may have been in a non-Jewish community, Luke was a meticulous historian and a learned man, who would have known some of the more widely circulating stories of the Jews, such as the story of Adam and Eve. Luke had to make sense of the fact that Jesus was indeed a Jew, and he would have been compelled to take into account some kind of Jewish heritage, so he chose to emphasize that which would be the most universal and inclusive of Gentiles. Likewise, other characteristics of Luke's account make comparatively few references to the Old Testament, which would have been strange and perhaps even unknown to his largely Gentile audience.

In the earliest parts of his Gospel, Luke tells many of the same miracle and healing stories contained in Mark, describing Jesus healing a leper, announcing the forgiveness of sins, and restoring life to the widow's son. Like Matthew, Luke deviates from Mark's Gospel and includes what he calls the Sermon on the Plain, which is Luke's equivalent to Matthew's description of the Sermon on the Mount. Luke is persistently concerned for the poor and the outcast, and his description of Jesus's sermon includes a series of warnings to the rich, fat, and mirthful (6:24–26). Chapter 7 introduces further incidents of Jesus's ministry in Galilee that are distinct from both Matthew and Mark and give us an indication of Luke's special interests: the faith of the Centurion's slave emphasizes and encourages the faith of a Gentile (7:1–10); the healing of the Widow's Son demonstrates Jesus's concern for a widow (7:11–17); the Ministering Woman in Chapter 8 stresses Jesus's readiness to help and be helped by women. Luke returns to Mark's Gospel for the subsequent miracles and healing stories.

The next Lucan section, "The Journey to Jerusalem," is the Gospel's longest, most loosely organized section (9.51–19:27). In this section, the narrative begins to move toward Jerusalem for the crucifixion, resurrection, and ascension—the ascension being the central event of Luke's Gospel. Contained in this section are some of the most well known parables in the entire New Testament, found only in Luke. These include the story of the Good Samaritan, a parable that reflects Luke's interest in Jesus's boundary-breaking behavior in associating with outcasts such as the Samaritans, a community once despised by Jews. Luke also includes a unique parable about Mary and Martha in which Jesus praises Mary, the female disciple who neglects her chores to listen to Jesus, and gently reproaches Martha, who is preoccupied by the traditional domestic duties of a woman. Also included are other well-known parables, such as those about the mustard seed and the rich fool storing his excess grain, and lessons on prayer, discipleship, and devotion—all of which stress the dangers of wealth and the importance of devotion to Jesus's way.

Chapter 15 is considered one of the greatest chapters of the New Testament. In it, Luke depicts three separate parables about being lost. The parable about the lost sheep among the ninety-nine found shows God's unending concern for the lost. The parable of the lost coin is similar, as is the famous story of the prodigal son, who is lost from his family and the standards of his father. The sheep, coin, and son are all found and returned to loving hands in their rightful places, which Luke uses to represent God's love and concern for the lost and forgotten. The loving concern exhibited toward these characters reflects the concern shown by Jesus, which the disciple must strive to emulate.

At a time in which most women were excluded from participating in public life in Rome, and were considered ritually impure for a substantial portion of their life according to Jewish custom, Luke's special concern for women and other outcasts of society is truly remarkable. His concern gives historians reason to think that there must have been a significant number of prominent female converts in Luke's community. Luke praises the courage of Mary, who rejoices over her fate to conceive the Son of God. From Luke, we also learn a bit more about Mary Magdalene, one of Jesus's closest disciples, who follows him to the tomb and is among the first to see that Jesus's body is missing. Luke tells us that Mary Magdalene was just one of many women who travel with Jesus and his male disciples in an age when the mixing of

sexes was virtually unheard of. Luke also tells us that these courageous women "provided for them out of their resources" (8:3). In
other words, women in the Gospel of Luke are largely responsible
for the finances of Jesus's followers. In Acts, Luke describes Lydia,
the wealthy merchant who provides for Paul, along with Pricilla,
Aquila, and Philip's four daughters, who are prophetesses (21:9).

Along with his concern and esteem for women, Luke also
shows preferential concern for the poor and the outcast. He repeatedly insists on the dangers of wealth and "abundance of possessions,"
but blesses and esteems those who are in fact impoverished (12:15).
These words must have been shocking to urban Gentile ears in a
society in which the overwhelming majority of the population was
destitute, impoverished, and enslaved—but now, suddenly, according to Jesus, blessed. While Luke takes great risks in his patriarchal,
hierarchical, and divisive society with his shocking words of inclusion
and universalism, he also makes concessions. Luke's Gospel and
Acts of the Apostles are the most pro-Roman works of the New
Testament. Luke is insistent on maintaining Pontius Pilate's innocence
in the crucifixion of the Jews and places all guilt in the hands of the
Jewish leaders. In Acts, during the stoning of Stephen, Stephen says
to a violent Jewish mob in Jerusalem, "You stiff-necked people,
uncircumcised in heart and ears, you are forever opposing the Holy
Spirit, just as your ancestors used to do. Which of the prophets did
your ancestors not persecute? They killed those who foretold the
coming of the Righteous One, and now you have become his betrayers
and murderers" (Acts 7:51–52).

Such loaded rhetoric is generally viewed as Luke's attempt
to persuade the Roman officials that the Christian Church, rapidly
growing in Gentile converts, was no threat to the Roman Empire.
This minority community wanted to appear on the side of the
Romans so as to give the empire, whose disregard for human life

has been nearly unrivaled in world history, no reason to pay them any heed or to regard them as a threat. The stories in Luke and Acts are politically structured to put all blame on the Jews, who were already a suspicious group with an alternative lifestyle to that of the Greco-Roman Empire, with its Greek philosophy and Roman Gods. This finger-pointing has indicated to historians that by the time of Luke, Christianity had become much more Gentile and less Jewish in its identity.

THE GOSPEL ACCORDING TO JOHN (JOHN)

INTRODUCTION

> *In the beginning was the Word, and the Word was with God, and the Word was God. He was in the beginning with God.*
>
> *(See* QUOTATIONS, *p. 205)*

The Fourth Gospel describes the mystery of the identity of Jesus. The Gospel According to John develops a Christology—an explanation of Christ's nature and origin—while leaving out much of the familiar material that runs through the synoptic Gospels of Matthew, Mark and Luke, including Jesus's short aphorisms and parables, references to Jesus's background, and proclamations about the kingdom of God. Whereas Mark's Gospel brings us the texture of first-century Palestine with a vivid, concrete, and earthy Jesus, John's Gospel is filled with long discourses describing Jesus's divinity. John takes us behind Jesus's ministry, where we get a glimpse of what it means to believe in Jesus as flesh of the eternal and living God, as the source of light and life, and for a believer to be a "Son of God." Though John's narrative diverges from the synoptic Gospels, it is indeed a Gospel, or a telling of good news. It includes the basics of Jesus's ministry—his preaching, miracles, trial, crucifixion, and resurrection. It is likely that John heard the details about these events from a very early oral source common to all the Gospels, but the freedom he uses to interpret these events helps us see clearly that all accounts of Jesus have come to us through the filter of interpretation. John may have been written a bit later than the synoptic Gospels, likely around 90 A.D. The actual author of John's Gospel was probably an interpreter of John, who was one of Jesus's original disciples.

John can be divided thematically into halves, preceded by a prologue and followed by an epilogue. The prologue is a poetic introduction that presents the outline of the narrative and the essence of John's theology. The first half of the Gospel can be characterized as a "Book of Signs." It tells of Jesus's ministry, focusing on seven major miracles worked by Jesus and the meaning and significance of those miracles. The second half of John has been called the "Book of Glory." In it, the narrative moves toward Jesus's glorification through crucifixion and resurrection. Finally, the book ends with an epilogue, most likely added to the Gospel by a later redactor, which tells of Jesus's appearance to the disciples after his resurrection.

Summary

The Gospel of John begins with a poetic hymn that tells the story of Jesus's origin, mission, and function. John says that Jesus is the incarnated Word of God, bringing "grace and truth," replacing the law given by Moses, and making God known in the world (1:17). The narrative opens with John the Baptist identifying himself as the fulfillment of Isaiah's prophecy; he will prepare the way for the

Lord. Indeed, when he meets Jesus, John testifies, "He is the Son of God" (1:34). The next day, hearing John's testimony, two disciples, including Andrew, begin to follow Jesus. Andrew brings his brother Simon to Jesus, who now accumulates several other followers as well. On the third day after Jesus's baptism, Jesus and his disciples attend a wedding at Cana in Galilee, where Jesus works a miracle, transforming water into wine. As Passover approaches, Jesus travels to Jerusalem, where he drives the money changers from the temple, charging them to "stop making my Father's house a marketplace" (2:16). A Pharisee named Nicodemus assumes that Jesus has come from God as a teacher, and Jesus tells him, in solemn, semipoetic lines, that he has been "born from above" (3:3) and that God has given "his only Son so that everyone who believes in him may not perish" (3:16). Jesus leaves Jerusalem and begins to baptize people in Judea. John the Baptist has continued his baptizing, and someone informs him that Jesus too has begun to baptize, assuming that John would be angry at the competition. The Baptist rejoices at the news, knowing that Jesus, as the Son of God, is the greater of the two, and that Jesus is the fulfillment of John's prophecy.

Jesus travels to Samaria, where he speaks in metaphors and figures of speech with a Samaritan woman and with his disciples. They do not always understand his metaphors, and take Jesus literally when he tells the woman that he has "living water" (4:10) and when he tells his disciples that "I have food to eat that you do not know about" (4:32). Eventually, the woman understands Jesus. Impressed by his knowledge of her past and by his message, she tells the other Samaritans that he is the Christ, meaning that he is the Messiah prophesied in Jewish scriptures. The Samaritans profess belief in him. Returning to Cana in Galilee, Jesus cures a boy who is at death's door. In Jerusalem once again for a festival, Jesus cures a sick man at the pool of Bethzatha and orders him to pick up his sleeping mat and walk around. As it is the Sabbath, when observant Jews do not carry objects outdoors, the Jews become angry with Jesus, and their anger only increases when Jesus explains that God is his father. Jesus delivers a long discourse, in which he announces that his words bring eternal life, and that rejection of Jesus in favor of the traditional laws is foolish, since Jesus represents the fulfillment of the Old Testament prophecies.

Returning to Galilee, Jesus is approached by a crowd of people looking for inspiration. To feed them, he works a miracle, providing food for 5,000 people with only five loaves of bread and two fish. Later that evening, Jesus's disciples are crossing the Sea of Galilee and are surprised to find Jesus walking across the water toward them. The next day, crowds of people come in search of Jesus, and he explains the significance of the miracle of the loaves: "I am the bread of life / no one can come to me unless it is granted by the Father" (6:35). Using the symbol of bread, Jesus explains that belief in him and in God, his father, will give eternal life. Many of his listeners disbelieve him, and Jesus teaches that belief in him is a foreordained gift from God: "Do not judge by appearances, but judge with right judgment" (6:65). Peter, however, remains with Jesus and professes his faith.

At the Feast of Booths, the Jewish holiday Sukkoth, Jesus returns to Jerusalem with the pilgrims and begins preaching in the temple. He urges the people not to hold his previous violation of the Sabbath against him, saying, "Do not judge by appearances, but judge with right judgment" (7:24). Many people wonder whether Jesus is the Christ, or Son of God, and the authorities want to arrest him but do not dare. The authorities bring him an adulterous woman and, in an attempt to entrap him, ask him whether or not she is guilty. Jesus responds, "Let anyone among you who is without sin be the first to throw a stone at her" (8:7). A long discourse ensues, in which Jesus responds to questions and accusations from the assembled people. Jesus predicts his own death and ascension, and explains that his authority comes from his origin in God and his fulfillment of the word of God. He accuses his listeners of being slaves to sin and, as sinners, of being illegitimate sons of God. Claiming to precede Abraham and to derive his glory from God, Jesus finally infuriates the crowd and barely escapes being stoned.

Jesus comes upon a man blind from birth and gives the man sight. The Pharisees are frustrated to realize that Jesus really has cured the man, who now professes faith in him. For their failure to believe, Jesus pronounces the Pharisees blind and teaches that he is the good shepherd, and that it is only through him that the sheep of Israel's flock shall be saved. Months pass, and at the Feast of Dedication, the Jewish holiday Hanukkah, Jesus is again confronted by the Jews in the temple, who ask whether or not he is the Christ. He responds by announcing that he is the Son of God, united with God. The crowd tries to stone him, but Jesus escapes Jerusalem.

Jesus is called to Bethany, the village where two of his devout followers, Mary and Martha, live with their brother Lazarus, who has fallen sick. Arriving in Bethany too late, Jesus finds Lazarus dead. He works a miracle to inspire belief in the observers, resurrecting Lazarus. Hearing of this spectacle, the Jewish leadership in Jerusalem, including the chief priests, decides to kill both Jesus and Lazarus. Nevertheless, Jesus travels to Jerusalem for Passover. He has foreseen his own death, as well as the salvation that he will bring through his sacrifice. Many of the Jews, despite witnessing signs of Jesus's divinity, continue to disbelieve, and Jesus decries their lack of faith.

At the Passover meal, or Seder, Jesus preaches extensively to the apostles. Through washing their feet, he teaches them that they must serve each other, saying, "I give you a new commandment, that you love one another" (13:34). Jesus stresses his unity with God: "I am in the Father, and the Father is in me" (14:10). Jesus foresees his own death and his betrayal by Judas. "I am going to the Father," he tells the apostles (14:28). Jesus assures the apostles that in Jesus's place, God will send an advocate, the Spirit of God, who will continue to dwell with the faithful, and who will lead them toward truth and salvation. He warns them that even after his death, they will continue to be persecuted, but that their ultimate salvation is imminent. Hearing this prophesy, the apostles finally express their firm belief in Jesus, and Jesus responds triumphantly, "I have conquered the world" (16:33). In a long, private prayer, Jesus addresses God directly, asking him to consecrate, glorify, and protect the faithful.

The narrative moves quickly toward its conclusion. Jesus is arrested by the soldiers whom Judas leads to him. He is brought first before the Jewish high priest, and then before Pontius Pilate, the Roman prefect. Pilate repeatedly interrogates Jesus, who refuses to confirm the allegation against him—that he has acted treasonably against Caesar by declaring himself King of the Jews. Pilate is reluctant to condemn Jesus, but the Jews agitate for Jesus's execution, and eventually Pilate consents. Jesus is crucified, and the soldiers cast lots to determine who will get his clothing. Pilate affixes a notice to the cross, reading "Jesus of Nazareth the King of the Jews" (19:19). Jesus dies, and to ensure his death, a solider pierces his side with a lance. Joseph of Arimathea and Nicodemus bury Jesus on a Friday.

On Sunday morning, Mary Magdalene comes to Jesus's grave and finds it empty. Jesus appears to her, and she brings the news of his resurrection to the disciples. Later that day, he appears to the disciples, whom he charges with the propagation of his message: "As the Father has sent me, so I send you" (20:21). Thomas is absent from the room, and he expresses doubt as to the resurrection until, a week later, Jesus reappears to him as well.

> *I have set you an example, that you also should do as I have done to you.*
>
> *(See* QUOTATIONS, *p. 208)*

ANALYSIS

For John, Jesus's miracles are not simply wonders to astonish on-lookers, but signs pointing to his glory that come from the presence of God within him. In the early stages of his ministry, John tells of an encounter between Jesus and a Samaritan woman at the well. At this time, the Samaritans were a group of people despised by the Jews, and casual conversation between men and women was taboo. Jesus asks the woman to fetch him water, but she misunderstands his words to mean literal water. Quickly, she learns that the water to which he refers is already in her presence, that Jesus is "a spring of water gushing up to eternal life," to which she replies, "Sir, give me this water so that I may never be thirsty" (4:14–15). This story is not a short parable, but an opportunity for Jesus to explain elaborately his personhood using life giving symbols characteristic of John's writing: water, words, bread, and light. John tells of this Samaritan woman leaving to then become a successful missionary of the "good news" in Samaria (4:42).

All the Gospel narratives diverge dramatically after the point at which Mark ends: the discovery of the empty tomb and the astonishment of the women. In Matthew, the women run to tell the disciples and are met by the risen Jesus on the way. In Luke, the women tell of their discovery of an empty tomb, but no one believes them until the resurrected Jesus makes a series of appearances before the other disciples. Here, in John's Gospel, Mary Magdalene tells

Peter and another disciple of the empty tomb, and, though she first mistakes him for a gardener, Jesus appears to her and discloses his identity. After his appearance to Mary, the risen Jesus appears to the disciples as a group, and John dramatizes the spiritual presence of Christ when Jesus breathes on his disciples. In both Hebrew and Greek, the word for "breath" is the same as that for "spirit."

The Gospel of John is perhaps the most difficult of the Gospels to understand, not because John is more complex than the others— Luke is perhaps the most technically difficult of the Gospels—but because it is so different from the other Gospels. Reading John in the context of the other Gospels can be a jarring experience, because the theological significance of the picture that John paints of Jesus's life is in many respects specific to John himself. Even John's solemn and poetic presentation is quite different from that of the other Gospels. The Gospel is also resistant to ecumenicalism, or attempts to reconcile varying religions; in the Gospel of John, Jesus declares, "I am the way, and the truth, and the life, No one comes to the Father except through me" (14:16).

Yet the Gospel of John also contains some of the most beautiful parts of the New Testament, such as Jesus's statement, "Let anyone among you who is without sin be the first to throw a stone at her" (8:7). Scholars believe that this story was circulating orally, and that church leaders were reluctant to add it into any of the synoptic Gospels because in official church doctrine, forgiveness for adultery was impossible. Instead of focusing on an official church, John's Gospel focuses on individual believers and their relationships to Jesus.

Perhaps the most striking aspect of John is its development of Christology, a discourse on the nature and origin of Jesus. Unlike Matthew and Luke, John is not interested in the details of Jesus's birth. Both Matthew and Luke stress that Jesus is born of a human mother who has somehow been visited by the Holy Spirit. John skips entirely the question of Jesus's conception. In fact, taken by itself, John offers no indication of any supernatural birth. Instead, John pictures Jesus as the Son of God in a sense that might be described as metaphorical. Jesus may well be a real human who possesses flesh and blood, but he is also the incarnation of the Divine Word. Indeed, just as Jesus himself is the Son of God, John speaks of Jesus giving his followers "power to become children of God"—descent from God is an attitude of faith and a gift of grace (1:12).

ACTS OF THE APOSTLES (ACTS)

INTRODUCTION

Acts of the Apostles, the second part of the work that begins with the Gospel According to Luke, is the story of the early church after Jesus's martyrdom. Like Luke, Acts is addressed to the unknown reader Theophilus, and in the introduction to Acts, it is made clear that it is a continuation of Luke: "In the first book, Theophilus, I wrote about all that Jesus did and taught from the beginning until the day he was taken up to heaven" (1:1–2). Second-century Christian tradition identifies the author of Luke and Acts as Luke, a traveling companion of the missionary Paul of Tarsus. Modern scholars agree that Acts and Luke should be credited to the same author, but have been more reluctant to identify him: the author most likely wrote between the years 80 and 90, and may indeed have been Paul's companion.

One of the perplexing problems surrounding the authorship of Acts is the narrator's changing voice and person. He generally speaks as an uninvolved third party, but sometimes lapses into the plural. Acts is certainly intended as a history of the early church, and it is the most complete and valuable history we have of the Christians in the first century. However, it is not necessarily historically reliable, either in terms of its depiction of the first-century development of Christian theology and religion, or in its description of the political history of the church. For instance, the author seems relatively shaky in his knowledge of Paul's theology. Whether or not it was intended to be a historically accurate text, Acts can be read as a devotional and instructional history, whose religious purpose remains unaffected by its inaccuracies. It depicts the story of the spread of Christianity, the growing distance between Christianity and Judaism, the move toward earthly concerns rather than apocalyptic expectations, and the triumph of the Christian message despite persecutions.

SUMMARY

Acts begins with Jesus's charge to the Twelve Apostles to spread the Gospel throughout the world. Peter serves as the leader of the apostles and the small congregation of the faithful in Jerusalem. Their first order of business is to elect Matthias as the twelfth apostle, replacing the traitor Judas Iscariot. During the year of Jesus's death and resurrection, the disciples are gathered for Pentecost, a religious holiday celebrating the grain harvest. The Holy Spirit descends upon them. As a result of the Holy Spirit's presence, they begin speaking other languages.

Peter delivers a sermon explaining the miracle. He says that the gift of tongues is given to prophets. Peter summarizes the life, crucifixion, and resurrection of Jesus. He gives scriptural proof that Jesus is the Messiah, the savior whom God promises in the Old Testament to send to save Jews from their adversity. Responding to Peter's sermon, 3,000 people are baptized into the Christian community—an idealized, thriving community characterized by prayer, brotherhood, common ownership, and sharing. A man named Barnabas is particularly praised for his generosity, and a couple that defrauds the church is stricken dead. Going to the temple to pray, Peter and John cure a crippled beggar. Peter tells a crowd the story of Jesus's persecution and his eventual resurrection, concluding with a reminder that the Jews are favored by God and a call to repentance. The Sadducee high priests of the temple, who do not believe in the resurrection of the dead, bring Peter and John before the Jewish high court, where Peter preaches the Gospel fearlessly. The court, which is called the Sanhedrin, recognizes that public opinion is in favor of the apostles and releases them with only a warning.

The high priest imprisons the apostles, but they are miraculously freed by an angel, and they continue their preaching. Brought again before the court, Peter leads the apostles in their defense, saying, "We must obey God rather than any human authority" (5:29). Influenced by the great sage Gamaliel, who warns, "[Y]ou will not be able to overthrow them—in that case you may even be found fighting against God," the court declines to execute the apostles, who continue preaching throughout Jerusalem (5:39).

The church divides into two groups. One group is the Hellenists, Christians who were born Jewish but who have a Greek cultural background. The other group is the Hebrews, the Christians who, like the apostles, were born into Jewish cultural backgrounds. The Hellenists feel discriminated against, so in response, the community of disciples elects seven leaders to account for the needs of the Hellenists. Foremost among these Christian Hellenist leaders is Stephen. A controversy ensues between Stephen and some Jews, who accuse him of heresy before the Sanhedrin. Stephen's accusers testify that "[t]his man never stops saying things against the holy place and the law" (7:13). In front of the Sanhedrin, Stephen delivers a long speech detailing the history of Jewish leadership in the Bible, concluding with a damning accusation: "Yet the Most High does not dwell in houses made with human hands. . . . You stiff-necked people . . . you are forever opposing the Holy Spirit, just as your ancestors used to do" (7:48–51).

Stephen is stoned to death, with the approval of a young man named Saul of Damascus, a vigorous persecutor of the Christians. Stephen is the first Christian martyr, a person who is killed as a result of defending the church. Saul is a Jewish leader who has been trying to wipe out the new community of Christians because he believes that they are trying to dismantle Jewish law. While traveling to persecute Christians, Saul is blinded by a light and hears the voice of Jesus asking, "Saul, Saul why do you persecute me?" (Acts 9:4). Saul then sets out to become the most relentless, brilliant, and bold missionary of Christianity that the church has ever known. He travels to the coast, performs miracles, preaches the Gospel, and converts Gentiles.

In a brief interlude, Acts recounts the miracles and speeches of Peter. Traveling to the coast, Peter cures a paralytic at Lydda and revives a woman at Joppa. In Caesarea, he says that he has received a message from God telling him that he "should not call anyone profane or unclean" (10:28). He deduces that he may associate with Gentiles, as "God shows no partiality, but in every nation anyone who fears him and does what is right is acceptable to him" (10:34). He therefore dines with the family of a Roman centurion named Cornelius, and they become the first Gentiles baptized by Peter. The church continues to shift its emphasis toward welcoming the Gentiles. Some of those who fled persecutions in Jerusalem arrive at the Syrian city of Antioch, where they begin to preach to the Greeks. Saul and Barnabas are among these people. Judea, meanwhile, is under the rule of King Herod Agrippa, who ruled from 41 to 44 A.D. Herod Agrippa introduces institutional persecution against the Christians and arrests Peter, who is miraculously freed from jail by an angel.

Barnabas and Saul, who is renamed Paul, depart on a missionary journey. In Cyprus, Paul blinds a magician, Elymas, who tries to prevent Paul from teaching. At Antioch in Pisidia, a central region in modern-day Turkey, Paul preaches to a Jewish congregation, telling his listeners about forgiveness of sins through faith in Jesus as the resurrected Messiah. Many listeners become converts, but many also contradict Paul, and the missionaries are expelled from the territory. At Iconium, too, they have some success until nonbelievers, including both Jews and Gentiles, drive them from town. At Lycaonia, Paul cures a cripple, and the local Gentiles take them for the pagan gods Zeus and Hermes before Paul is able to convince them otherwise. As usual, however, the missionaries are chased from town, and Paul is nearly stoned to death. The two make their way back to Antioch in Syria, preaching the whole way. A controversy arises as a result of their missionary activities among the Gentiles, and Paul and Barnabas journey to Jerusalem for a debate of church leaders.

At the debate, traditional Jewish Christians argue that, to become a Christian, one must first convert to Judaism and become circumcised. Paul and Barnabas are strong supporters of expanding the church among Gentiles. Peter and James, leaders of the Jewish Christians in Jerusalem, decide in favor of Paul's perspective, arguing that they should preserve the community of believers and "not trouble those Gentiles who are turning to God" (15:19). Only a minimal adherence to the law is required of Christian Gentiles. Paul separates from Barnabas and, together with another disciple, Silas, sets out in Macedonia. Local Gentiles are angry at their exorcism of a spirit from a soothsayer slave, which deprives her of the ability to tell the future. They imprison Paul and Silas. An earthquake shakes the prison cell, and the missionaries are quickly released.

In Greece, Paul meets with mixed success, converting some but meeting opposition from many Jews and some Gentiles. In Athens, Paul speaks at the public forum, the Areopagus, contextualizing Christianity within Greek beliefs. From Athens, Paul travels to Corinth, where he turns away from the Jews in despair and preaches almost entirely to the Gentiles with great success. He also attracts his faithful disciples Aquila and Priscilla. The Jews take Paul before the governor of the region to accuse him, but the governor refuses to adjudicate a matter of religious faith. Paul, after a brief return to Antioch, continues to work his way through Greece, establishing the church in Ephesus and working great miracles. He leaves Ephesus after a mass riot instigated by the silversmiths, who are concerned that Paul's preaching against pagan idolatry will ruin their trade.

Paul travels onward and stops to revive a dead man in Troas. Paul sends for the Christian elders of Ephesus, and in an emotional speech he reminds them of his faithful service to them and warns them of the persecution that might begin. The Holy Spirit urges him to travel to Jerusalem, where he himself expects to be persecuted and possibly killed. In Jerusalem, Paul meets with James and the church leaders, who are concerned that Paul appears to have been urging Christians not to follow Jewish law. They plan for Paul to make a public show of worship at the temple, to indicate that he continues to adhere to Jewish law. In the temple, however, Jews seize him, accusing him of profaning the temple and preaching against the law. Paul tells the crowd his personal history. He relates the stories of his past persecution of Christians, his miraculous vision of Christ, and his conversion to Christianity and mission to preach to the Gentiles.

The crowd becomes outraged, and the Roman tribune seizes Paul and flogs him. The tribune then has him brought before the Jewish high court, the Sanhedrin, where Paul creates dissent by setting the two factions in the court, the Pharisees and the Sadducees, against each other. The tribune saves Paul from the ensuing riot, and, hearing of a Jewish plot against Paul's life, sends him for his own protection to Felix, the governor of Palestine, in Caesarea. At the trial in Caesarea, Paul professes to worship God and adhere to Jewish law. He claims that it is only because of his belief in the resurrection of the dead—a belief not shared by the Sadducees—that he is on trial. Hearing that Paul collects and distributes alms, Felix holds him in jail for two years, hoping for a bribe. After Felix's death, Paul is tried before the new governor, Festus. Paul appeals to Caesar's judgment, and Festus—who does not believe Paul guilty, but who wants to appease the Jews calling for his execution—resolves to send him to Caesar, in Rome. First, however, Paul is brought before Herod Agrippa, the Jewish puppet-king of Palestine. Again, Paul recounts the story of his vision of Jesus and conversion to Christianity, and argues that his missionary activity is merely a fulfillment of Jewish hopes and Old Testament prophecies. King Herod Agrippa is impressed, but Paul is sent to Rome. On the way to Rome, Paul's ship is wrecked, and through a series of sailing mishaps it takes months to arrive at Rome. Awaiting his hearing at Rome, Paul begins to spread the Gospel to the Roman Jews, who disbelieve him. He turns his emphasis again toward the Gentiles, and as Acts ends, Paul is in Rome, "teaching about the Lord Jesus Christ with all boldness and without hindrance" (28:31).

ANALYSIS

Acts of the Apostles demonstrates the importance of missionary work in the early church. The book begins with the appearance of the resurrected Jesus to his disciples, who are anxious for the final redemption. The apostles demand of Jesus, "Lord, is this the time when you will restore the kingdom to Israel?" (1:6). Jesus responds by charging them to concern themselves not with the Apocalypse, but with spreading the Gospel on Earth: "It is not for you to know the times or periods that the Father has set by his own authority. But you will receive power when the Holy Spirit has come upon you; and you will be my witnesses in Jerusalem, and in all Judea and Samaria, and to the ends of the earth" (1:7–8). It is through Paul, the great early missionary of the church, that Acts dramatizes the fulfillment of Jesus's command, the spreading of the Gospel across the known world. Paul dominates the second half of Acts and, more than any other figure, dictates the trajectory of the church's rise. Acts begins with Peter and the apostles in Jerusalem; it ends, years later, with Paul in Rome. Paul's final words are an apt summary of the direction in which he leads the missionary church in the vital first decades of its existence: "Let it be known to you then," he says to the Jews of Rome, "that this salvation of God has been sent to the Gentiles; they will listen" (28:28).

The ending of Acts in Rome foreshadows the eventual transition of the church to that city. Acts is the story of the church's turn away from Jerusalem and toward Antioch, Ephesus, and Rome. Acts is filled with stories and speeches, but the dramatic arc that connects all of Acts of the Apostles is the church's move, driven by Paul, toward a split with Judaism and an emphasis on converting Gentiles. It is in that move that Christianity becomes its own distinct religion. Jesus and his followers consider themselves Jews, and Jesus's message and teachings are the fulfillment of Jewish prophecies. It is evident from the first chapters of Acts that, in the first years after Jesus's ascension, the apostles and their followers continued to consider themselves Jews, and to follow Jewish law.

Peter and John, both of whom consider Jews the chosen people of God, are on their way to worship in the Jewish temple when they encounter the cripple. "You are the descendents of the prophets," Peter tells a Jewish audience, "and of the covenant that God gave to your ancestors. . . . When God raised up his servant [Jesus], he sent him first to you" (3:25–26).

The early church controversy between the Hellenists and the Hebrews introduces the first dissent within the church itself. The Hellenists are Jewish adherents to Jesus who were born into a Greek cultural background. They feel that the Hebrews, Jewish Christians who were born into a Jewish cultural background and who adhere strictly to Jewish law, are discriminating against them. The apostles and disciples decide that unity is more important than conformity, and they accept the position of the Hellenists, even appointing Stephen and six others to minister to the Hellenists in the church. When Stephen breaks with Jewish tradition, however, he shows how Christianity is becoming increasingly incompatible with Judaism. Although Stephen is stoned to death, the Hellenists continue to move away from the Jewish focus of the church, baptizing Samaritans and an Ethiopian. A turning point for the church occurs when Peter himself receives a message from God: "God has shown me that I must not call anyone profane or unclean" (10:28). The message challenges one of the fundamental aspects of Judaism, the idea that Jews are a special population chosen by God. But God's message to Peter indicates that Gentiles are no less clean than Jews, and therefore that "God has given even to the Gentiles the repentance that leads to life" (11:18).

The church in Antioch is founded immediately after the Jerusalem elders accept Peter's rationale for baptizing a Gentile, thus laying the foundation for the Antioch church to become dominated by Gentile Christians. It also indicates the increasing degree to which followers of Jesus Christ are non-Jewish. The acceptance of Gentiles gives impetus to the move away from Jewish law and Judaism, and it signals the beginning of the move away from Jerusalem. In fact, at Antioch the disciples are first called Christians rather than Jews. Paul becomes the great Christian missionary to the Gentiles, traveling throughout Greece and Asia Minor and, while receiving little welcome from the Jews, recruiting many Gentiles to the church. Paul and Barnabus say, "It was necessary that the word of God should be spoken first to you. Since you reject it and judge yourselves to be unworthy of eternal life, we are now turning to the Gentiles" (13:46).

The New Testament texts are not monolithic, or conveying only a single, objective perspective. The Book of Acts reveals that early Christianity was a highly dynamic movement, full of doctrinal and theological differences. Acts functions as a historical text in allowing us a unique insight into the transition of Christianity from a Jewish sect into its own religion. The controversies over adherence to Jewish law, the role of Gentiles within the church, and the relationship of the Diaspora communities to the Jerusalem community make it possible to understand Paul's letters, which comprise a later part of the New Testament. Acts describes the beginning of the process by which the faith of a few followers grew into a church that dominated Europe for more than 1,000 years.

THE LETTER OF PAUL TO THE ROMANS (ROMANS)

INTRODUCTION

Of the twenty-seven books in the New Testament, fourteen have traditionally been attributed to the great missionary Paul of Tarsus. These fourteen books all take the form of letters addressed to a given individual or community. In the traditional canonical ordering of the New Testament, these fourteen books are arranged in a block following Acts, and separated into three groups: the nine letters addressed to communities, the four letters addressed to individuals, and Hebrews. Within each grouping, the traditional canonical system orders the books according to length. Thus, a traditional New Testament arrangement will list the books as follows: Romans, 1 and 2 Corinthians, Galatians, Ephesians, Philippians, Colossians, 1 and 2 Thessalonians, 1 and 2 Timothy, Titus, Philemon, and Hebrews. This book addresses only a few of the most important letters: Romans, 1 and 2 Corinthians, and Ephesians. Modern scholars agree with the traditional second-century Christian belief that seven of these New Testament letters were almost certainly written by Paul himself: 1 Thessalonians, Galatians, Philippians, Philemon, 1 and 2 Corinthians, and Romans. These letters were most likely written during the height of Paul's missionary activity, between 50 and 58 A.D., making them the earliest surviving Christian documents—they predate the earliest of the Gospels, Mark, by at least ten years.

During the winter of 57–58 A.D., Paul was in the Greek city of Corinth. From Corinth, he wrote the longest single letter in the New Testament, which he addressed to "God's beloved in Rome" (1:7). Like most New Testament letters, this letter is known by the name of the recipients, the Romans. Paul's letters tended to be written in response to specific crises. For instance, 1 Corinthians was written to reprove the Christian community in Corinth for its internal divisions and for its immoral sexual practices. But Romans is remarkably devoid of this kind of specificity, addressing broad questions of theology rather than specific questions of con-temporary practice. Whereas other Pauline letters—2 Corinthians, for instance—are full of impassioned rhetoric and personal pleas, Romans is written in a solemn and restrained tone. Perhaps this solemnity can be explained by timing: Romans was the last written of the seven New Testament letters that modern scholars attribute to Paul, and has been seen as a summary of Paul's thought, composed as his career moved toward its conclusion. But it is also true that, as opposed to the Corinthian church, the Roman church was not founded by Paul himself. At the time when he wrote Romans, Paul had never visited Rome, although Chapter 16 of Romans does indicate that he had acquaintances there. Writing to a community largely composed of strangers, then, Paul may have felt compelled to use the restrained and magisterial declarations of Roman style, rather than the impassioned pleas and parental sternness that permeate his letters to the churches at Corinth.

SUMMARY

Because he is not personally familiar with the Roman church, Paul begins his letter by introducing himself. He has been "called to be an apostle," and his mission is "to bring about the obedience of faith among all the Gentiles" (1:1–5). Paul follows his introduction with a flattering greeting to the Roman church, and expresses his desire to preach in Rome someday. Paul gives a summary of the theme of his letter: "The Gospel . . . is the power of God for salvation to everyone who has faith, to the Jew first and also to the Greek. For in it the righteousness of God is revealed through faith for faith" (1:16–17).

Paul begins with a discussion of the state of humanity before the possibility of salvation through faith in Jesus. He tells how Gentiles worshipped idols, disdaining devotion to God, and how Jews failed to follow the law properly, acting hypocritically by proclaiming allegiance to Jewish law while surreptitiously sinning. Paul says that God's ancestral promise to the Jews, symbolized by circumcision, does not bring automatic salvation: "A person is a Jew who is one inwardly, and real circumcision is a matter of the heart—it is spiritual" (2:29). Paul concludes, "We have already charged that all, both Jews and Greeks, are under the power of sin" (3:9).

Paul teaches that salvation from sin is only possible through faith. Paul cites the example of the biblical patriarch Abraham, who received God's blessing and passed it on to his descendents through "the righteousness of faith" (4:13). The free gift of grace, Paul continues, unearned and undeserved, is a product of God's love manifested toward the unworthy. Whereas Adam's fall brought sin and death into the world, Jesus's sacrifice brought grace and life. The importance of baptism, Paul explains, is that baptism initiates a new life of grace and purity: the sinner symbolically dies, baptized into the death of Jesus, and the person who emerges is "dead to sin and alive to God in Christ Jesus" (6:11). Christians, then, must be governed by holiness, not by sin: holiness alone will lead to eternal life. Jewish law ceases to be binding: the law arouses sinful passions, and as beings dead to sin, Christians become dead to the law. Paul urges the Romans to live not "according to the flesh" but rather by the Spirit (8:4). Through the Spirit, all believers become spiritual children of God, called by God to glory. This potential is a source of strength for the Christian: "If God is for us, who is against us?" (8:31).

Paul's next topic is the problem of reconciling the doctrine of salvation through faith in Christ with the Old Testament promise of the salvation of the Jewish people. This section begins with a lamentation, as Paul, who was himself born a Jew, expresses his wish to help the Israelites, the supposed firstborn children of God. But he goes on to explain that the Christian covenant of grace is by no means a betrayal of Abraham's covenant with God. Those who have faith in Jesus, who believe "with the heart," are "children of the promise," the spiritual children of Israel (10:10, 9:8). The genetic children of Israel, the Jews, stumbled when they mistook Jewish law for the means to salvation. But the Jews have not been entirely cast aside. Paul teaches that eventually the Jews will come to express faith in Jesus, enabling God to keep his original promise to them.

Finished with his exposition of Christian doctrine, Paul embarks upon a lengthy exhortation to the Romans, advising them on the proper means of living a Christian life. Harmony, humility, and love are his main concerns. He urges charity, forbearance, and submission. Paul returns to the apocalyptic theme on which he dwells in his other letters. He says that it is doubly important to act righteously in an apocalyptic age. In a long segment, Paul mandates tolerance and freedom of religious conscience within the church. The strong in faith are not to judge and reject the weak in faith— that is, those who have given up Jewish law are to accept the observances of those who continue to practice Jewish law. Paul finishes this section with a set of Old Testament quotations about the worship of God spreading among all nations. Paul concludes his letter with a section in which he discusses his own ministry, proving his authority through a discussion of his credentials: "I have reason to boast of my work for God" (15:17). He informs the Romans that he is preparing to bring the contributions of the Greek and Macedonian churches to Jerusalem, where he speculates that he might run into difficulties. Chapter 16 contains a long list of greetings, which many scholars believe were added by a later editor. Paul sends the greetings to the Roman Christians, warning the Romans to be wary of "those who cause dissensions and offenses" (16:17).

ANALYSIS

The period during which Paul wrote his letters was traumatic for the new church. Christianity had not yet evolved into a distinct religion with a hierarchy of authority and a defined dogma. Christianity, in its earliest years, was an offshoot of Judaism. Believers in Jesus, including all of the Twelve Apostles, were generally born Jewish and identified themselves as Jews who believed that the Old Testament prophecies had reached their fulfillment in Jesus. Indeed, the term "Christians" did not appear until Paul's ministry at Antioch, decades after Jesus's crucifixion. The church was not a single, unified body governed by a central authority, but, rather, a conglomeration of individual communities, often separated by large distances, which depended for spiritual authority on local preachers or traveling missionaries, like Paul. Christians in the decades after Jesus lived in constant fear of persecution and constant expectation of the second coming, Jesus's triumphant return to Earth during which he would save the faithful.

The letters that Paul wrote respond to these conditions of the early church. He addresses them to specific communities, most of which had been established by Paul himself. In an era when travel was slow and long-distance communication was difficult, Paul's letters were a means of preserving his spirit in a community once he had left, or of instructing a community from a distance. The aim of the letters was to inspire unity among believers and to instruct the faithful on difficult points of doctrine. The letters are highly indi-vidualized, responding to the specific problems of the community to which they are addressed. By and large, with the possible exception of the letter to the Romans, Paul's letters show little evidence that they were intended to endure as permanent documents. Paul, like other early Christians, expected an imminent Second Coming, and he wrote his letters to address immediate problems rather than to establish a lasting apparatus to perpetuate the church.

The four Gospels can be viewed as a history of the birth of faith. The Gospels all follow a similar pattern. They describe Jesus working miracles and preaching, but failing to convince many people of his divinity until his resurrection. The triumphant moment in the Gospels comes when the apostles witness the reborn Jesus and have their faith confirmed. The entire story of the Gospels is designed to stress the importance of faith for the Christian. Indeed, practically the only factor that separated these early Christians from the nonbelieving Jews was faith in Jesus. Nowhere in the Gospels, however, is the opposition between faith and law made so clear as in Romans. Paul elevates the role of faith, describing it as the sole means by which people can attain salvation. Through Jesus's self-sacrifice, Paul teaches, God gave men the free gift of a covenant of salvation. It is only by faith in Jesus that one attains salvation.

THE FIRST LETTER OF PAUL TO THE CORINTHIANS (1 CORINTHIANS)

INTRODUCTION

There is a general consensus among scholars that 1 Corinthians was written by the important early Christian missionary Paul of Tarsus. In late 56 or early 57 A.D., Paul was in the city of Ephesus in Asia Minor. From there, writing with his collaborator Sosthenes, he addressed a series of letters to the Greek city of Corinth, which he had visited between 50 and 52 A.D., and where he had converted both Jews and Gentiles to the Christian faith. Corinth was located on the isthmus connecting the Peloponnesian peninsula to the Greek mainland, and its advantageous location allowed it to become a prosperous merchant city. Prosperity, however, brought pagan hedonism. Corinth developed a reputation, widespread throughout the ancient world, for sexual license. Paul's letters to the Christians at Corinth address his concern over a pressing issue: the rampant immorality associated with the paganism of Corinth. This immorality had begun to infect the Corinthian church. Paul was deeply concerned for the spiritual health of the Corinthian church, which had been deprived of his guidance for several years. As a result, Paul corresponded at greater length with the Corinthian church than with any of the other communities that he established. The New Testament preserves two of these letters, 1 and 2 Corinthians, and makes reference to at least one other lost letter (1 Cor. 5:9).

SUMMARY

Paul begins 1 Corinthians with a greeting to "the church of God that is in Corinth," in which he offers thanks for the faith and strength of the Corinthian church (1:2). He immediately begins, however, to list and address the problems that plague that church. The first problem, to which he devotes almost four chapters, concerns factionalism within the church. Paul has heard that the Corinthian church has divided itself according to the various preachers of the Gospel: "each of you says, 'I belong to Paul,' or 'I belong to Apollos,' or 'I belong to Cephas,' or 'I belong to Christ'" (1:12). Paul stresses that each preacher of the Gospel is merely a servant of Jesus, and that all believers should be united in Jesus. The faithful should put aside their differences and remember that "[a]ll things are yours. . . . You belong to Christ, and Christ belongs to God" (3:23). The place of the preachers is not to establish themselves as leaders among men; instead, "[p]eople should think of us as servants of Christ" (4:1).

Paul enumerates various immoral tendencies of the Corinthian Christians. He cautions them to condemn sexual immorality within the church. Membership in the community of the faithful, he teaches, means that the church faithful must adjudicate moral matters amongst themselves, chastising and expelling sinners. In response to questions put to him about specific confusions over religious practice, Paul sets forth a principle that becomes embedded in church doctrine: "To the unmarried . . . I say: it is well for them to remain unmarried as I am. But if they are not practicing self-control, they should marry" (7:8–9). Paul advocates freedom of conscience within the bounds of faith. He does not mandate circumcision, although many early Christians, who were practically all Jewish, assumed that circumcision was a prerequisite for conversion to Christianity. Paul declares it permissible to eat food dedicated to false gods, provided that one does not compromise the conscience of another Christian by doing so.

In a break from his instruction, Paul spends Chapter 9 discussing his own case. He sees himself as a man who has sacrificed everything to preach the Gospel, forgoing material comfort and becoming all things to all people. Returning to his moral instruction, Paul invokes the example of the ancient Israelites, who were punished for their immorality and faithlessness, and exhorts the Corinthians to avoid idolatrous worship and sexual immorality. He explains to them that while it is not forbidden to eat certain foods, it is best to avoid offending people and to respect the consciences of others. Paul then speaks on public worship. He says that women must cover their heads during prayer, while men must pray with heads bared. When the Lord's Supper is commemorated, it must be celebrated in true communal fashion, and must be preceded by careful self-inspection.

In Chapters 12 and 14, Paul speaks of the regulation of spiritual gifts in the church of believers. There are many instances in the Corinthian church of people prophesying and speaking in tongues. These spiritual gifts are important because they help to strengthen the community. All gifts, and all believers, are indispensable to the church. Each believer is a part of the incarnated body of Jesus, and each fulfills his or her own particular function. But Paul prioritizes prophecy, with its clarity of message, over speaking in tongues, which is generally indecipherable and therefore cannot provide instruction to the community. Paul interrupts this discussion of spiritual gifts with Chapter 13, which has become known as the Hymn to Love, in which he expounds upon the importance of love: "And now faith, hope, and love abide, these three; and the greatest of these is love" (13:13).

Paul moves toward his conclusion with an exposition on the doctrinal question of the resurrection of the dead. He reminds the Corinthians of the core Christian doctrine. The resurrection of Jesus, he insists, is a cardinal point of the Christian faith. The future resurrection of all the dead stems from Jesus's own resurrection, and it is the future resurrection—the promise of eternal life—that makes Christian sacrifice meaningful: "If the dead are not raised, Let us eat and drink, for tomorrow we die" (15:33). Paul explains the nature of resurrection, noting that the physical body will not be resurrected. Rather, it is the spiritual body that is immortal. The immortality of the spiritual body signifies the true victory of faith over death, and Paul concludes, "Thanks be to God, who gives us the victory through our Lord Jesus Christ" (15:57). Finally, 1 Corinthians ends with Paul's instruction to the Corinthians to take up a collection for the benefit of the poor in Jerusalem. He expresses his hope that he will be able to visit Corinth soon, and in the meanwhile urges the Corinthians to accept his emissary Timothy with open arms. He charges them to "[k]eep alert, stand firm in your faith, be courageous, be strong. Let all that you do be done in love" (16:13–14).

ANALYSIS

In 1 Corinthians, through the issues that he chooses to address, Paul provides us with historical insight into the early Christian Church. It was a church without any single supreme authority. The missionaries and preachers who spread the Gospel in the decades after Jesus were by no means homogenous in their approaches to Christian doctrine and practice. Paul speaks of divisions in the church at Corinth that stem from perceived differences in the Gospel as preached by various missionaries. It seems that Paul, Apollos, and Cephas (the Aramaic name given to Peter) each had adherents in the Corinthian church. It is possible that the Christians at Corinth, recent converts who were inadequately instructed in Christianity, simply misunderstood the missionaries and believed doctrinal differences to exist. It is also possible that there were actual important differences between the Christianity of Peter and that of Paul. Instances of disagreements between early Christian leaders are both implicit and explicit in The New Testament. For instance, in Acts 15, it is evident that the apostles Peter and James are more conservative than Paul with regard to adhering to Jewish law. But it is also true that in Corinthians, Paul addresses a group of people with little knowledge of Paul's Jewish culture. A certain amount of confusion was probably inevitable.

Paul's letter is remarkable in that it exhorts the Corinthians toward unity rather than ideological division. He does not mandate resolving whatever differences may exist between the factions of the Corinthian church. Rather, he reminds them of the all-important unity that binds them and supersedes their differences. Throughout 1 Corinthians, the themes of unity and the importance of freedom of conscience within certain moral boundaries are constantly stressed. This freedom of conscience extends from doctrinal issues to questions of practice: for instance, Paul permits the Corinthians to eat food sacrificed to idols (10:26–27), in direct defiance of the principle established by the church leaders in Jerusalem (Acts 15:28–29). In his discussion of the various spiritual gifts granted to the faithful, Paul returns again to the theme of unity through diversity: "Now there are varieties of gifts, but the same Spirit; and there are varieties of services, but the same Lord" (12:4–5).

Paul's great commandment is to love. He hopes that love will bind the community together despite its differences, and lead people to achieve faith and godliness in anticipation of the imminent Second Coming. Paul attempts to unify the church by accepting varying beliefs and practices, but his emphasis on unity does not reflect any willingness to compromise his religious faith. Paul's accepting attitude has limitations, and 1 Corinthians is filled with Paul's righteous indignation. He does not hesitate to "say this to your shame" to the Corinthians, nor to chastise them for their moral misdeeds (15:34). In this letter, Paul assumes the voice of a stern but loving parent. He says, "In Christ Jesus I became your father" (4:15), and he tells the Corinthians, "I fed you with milk" (3:2). The family of believers is open to all who are faithful. Unlike many of the early Christians, Paul is willing to accept Gentile as well as Jew: "For in the one Spirit we were all baptized into one body . . . slaves or free" (12:13). But acceptance does not mean tolerance of repeated misdeeds and the refusal to repent: "Drive out the wicked person from among you" (5:13).

THE SECOND LETTER OF PAUL TO THE CORINTHIANS (2 CORINTHIANS)

INTRODUCTION

> *For in Christ Jesus you are all children of God through faith. As many of you as were baptized into Christ have clothed yourselves with Christ.*
> *(See* QUOTATIONS, *p. 206)*

The book known as 2 Corinthians is one of the fourteen New Testament letters that have traditionally been attributed to Paul,

the great early Christian missionary preacher. While the authorship of many of these letters has been debated by modern scholars,
there is a nearly unanimous consensus that 2 Corinthians was
written by Paul. However, it was probably not written in the
same form in which it appears today. Most scholars agree that
2 Corinthians is a combination of several letters written by Paul
to the community of Christian believers in the Greek city of
Corinth. These letters would have been written at intervals of
several months.

Following the sending of 1 Corinthians, Paul's disciple,
Timothy, visited Corinth, and discovered that the situation there
had not improved (Acts 19:21–22). Responding to this emergency,
Paul paid an immediate visit to Corinth. He later refers to this visit
as "painful" (2 Cor. 2:1). Apparently, an anonymous adversary
publicly confronted Paul and undermined his authority. Whereas
Paul had threatened to come to Corinth "with a stick" (1 Cor.
4:21), he was perceived on this later occasion as unimpressive and
timid "(2 Cor. 10:1). Leaving Corinth, Paul decided not to visit
again "until he had sent a letter "in much distress and anguish of
the heart" (2 Cor. 2:4). It is possible that this letter has been lost. It
is also possible that the letter was preserved and incorporated into
the main body of 2 Corinthians as Chapters 10–13, an incongru-
ous section whose shift in tone from the optimism of the preceding
chapters is jarring, and which seems to rehash a controversy that
has already been resolved. Soon after the Corinthians received this
agonized letter, Titus, another disciple of Paul, visited Corinth,
and found the community repentant as a result of Paul's letter (2
Cor. 7:5–13). Returning to Paul in Macedonia, Titus brought the
happy news. In the early fall of 57 A.D., rejoicing at the news of the
Corinthian repentance, Paul then wrote the letter to the church at
Corinth that became 2 Corinthians.

SUMMARY

The letter that is 2 Corinthians begins with a long salutation and prayer of thanksgiving (1:1–11). Paul, writing with his disciple Timothy, thanks God for the encouragement he has received despite all the suffering he has recently undergone. The body of the letter begins with Paul's assertion that his behavior, especially toward the Corinthian church, has been inspired by the grace of God. His decision not to visit the Corinthians, and instead to write them a chastising letter "in much distress and anguish of the heart," is a decision made through God's grace (2:4). The agonized letter is intended not "to cause you pain, but to let you know the abundant love that I have for you" (2:4). He demonstrates this love by urging the repentant community to show love and forgiveness to the unnamed adversary who shamed Paul on the occasion of his previous, unsuccessful visit.

Paul spends much of the body of the letter justifying his own apostolic calling. As an envoy of God, spreading the Gospel of God, Paul is empowered to speak "with great boldness" (3:12). Paul takes pride in his ministry. His pride and fearlessness persist despite the many hardships to which he has been subjected as an apostle. Guided by faith, Paul does not hesitate to devote his life to the benefit of his human flock. However oppressed the ministers of God may be, Paul remembers that "we have a building from God," and that he will eventually be rewarded (5:1). Just as God will judge him justly, Paul asks the Corinthians to judge him justly: "We ourselves are well known to God, and I hope that we are also well known to your consciences" (5:11). Paul hopes to become "the righteousness of God," charged with the spreading of the Gospel, and he urges the Corinthians to be attentive to this Gospel (5:21). He concludes the section on the importance and authenticity of his calling with a brilliant evocation of the paradoxical status of the oppressed minister of God.

Paul's "heart is wide open" to the Corinthians, and he speaks honestly about his personal joy in his calling (6:11). He asks the Corinthians to reciprocally open their hearts, to treat him honestly, and to judge him fairly. After a brief interlude in which Paul pauses to warn the Corinthians against association with unbelievers, Paul continues with words of encouragement. Titus has told him of the Corinthian church's positive response to the agonized letter of chastisement that Paul sent them. Through the distress they felt at receiving his letter, they were led to repentance. Paul is now confident in the Corinthian church, and as a result he makes a request of them. In Chapters 8–9, he speaks of taking up a collection to support the church in Jerusalem, and urges the Corinthians to give generously: "As you excel in everything—in faith, in speech, in knowledge, in utmost eagerness, and in our love for you—so we want you to excel also in this generous undertaking" (8:7).

It has been suggested that Chapters 10–13 are the remnants of the agonized letter that Paul earlier sent to the Corinthians. Certainly, these chapters represent an abrupt shift from the triumphant tone of reconciliation in Chapters 7–9: Chapters 10–13 are a vehement defense of Paul's apostolic calling, and a strong repudiation of his critics. Paul speaks at length of the hardships he has undergone for the sake of his ministry: "I am a better one: with far greater labors, far more imprisonments, with countless floggings, and often near death" (11:23). Paul asserts that he is not inferior in importance even to the "super-apostles," the twelve original disciples appointed by Jesus. The favor of God is equally upon him, and he says that he has displayed "utmost patience, signs and wonders and mighty works" (12:12). Implicit is the idea that, since Paul is qualified as an apostle, the Corinthians should respect him and pay attention to his sermons. He is sending them this difficult letter, he tells them, "so that when I come, I may not have to be severe in using the authority that the Lord has given me for building up and not tearing down" (13:10). In conclusion, Paul wishes the Corinthians joy, communal harmony, and peace.

ANALYSIS

Modern scholars generally agree that at least seven New Testament letters can be attributed with reasonable certainty to Paul. Through his letters, and through his biography in Acts, Paul has become the most developed character in the New Testament. He exists for us not just as a towering religious figure, but as a deeply human personality. The letters give a startlingly clear picture of Paul—in his anger, despair, and triumph—throughout the many difficulties and victories he encounters during his ministry. Of all the New Testament books, 2 Corinthians is probably the most intensely personal. It is Paul's cry from the heart, a testimony to his devoted ministry to his communities of converts, but it is also revelatory of his human imperfections, his deep-seated insecurity and his quick temper.

Paul is a gifted correspondent. He has a talent for producing concise epigrams, such as "what can be seen is temporary, but what cannot be seen is eternal" (4:18). He is also a great poet. As he demonstrates in 2 Corinthians, he can be both gentle and severe at the same time. At one point, he says, "I am overjoyed in all our affliction" (7:4); later, he says, "If I come again, I will not be resilient" (13:2). He can also be self-effacingly humble and expansively boastful in the same breath, making comments such as, "I am not at all inferior to these super-apostles, even though I am nothing" (12:11).

In both 1 and 2 Corinthians, Paul spends a good deal of time rehearsing his qualifications for ministry and the extent of his martyrdom. Paul frequently seems insecure, perhaps as a result of the loose hierarchy of the early church. Paul may consider himself the equal of the "super-apostles," the twelve disciples appointed by Jesus himself as the heads of the church, but the fact remains that he is not one of the original apostles. Paul develops the term "super-apostle" to account for calling himself simply an "apostle," a title to which his claim was not well established. Paul believes that his epiphany on the road to Damascus in Acts 9 is as important a personal encounter with Jesus as any revelation experienced by the original Twelve Apostles. At one point, Paul's ministry is contrasted with that of Peter, the greatest of the original Twelve Apostles—a moment that could not have been comfortable for Paul (1 Cor. 1:12). Paul's dedication throughout the Corinthian correspondence to proving his equality with the "super-apostles" may well be a response to the implicit challenge to his apostolic station.

THE REVELATION TO JOHN (REVELATION)

INTRODUCTION

The Book of Revelation is strikingly different from the rest of the New Testament. It is populated by winged and wild creatures, locust plagues, and seven-headed beasts. Revelation is filled with obscure and fantastic symbolism, and it teems with mystical references. However, it lacks any real internal structure. Unlike the other New Testament books, which tend to mix narrative with sermon-style preaching, Revelation is essentially a long, uninterrupted record of a mystical vision, offering little interpretation for its intricate symbols. Revelation has been read for thousands of years as a code that, properly interpreted, can reveal the secrets of history and the end of the world. The numbers and symbols in Revelation have been read into any number of traumatic events in ancient and modern history.

Revelation was a product of this time of early growth and confusion, but also of a long Jewish tradition of apocalyptic literature. The Old Testament books of Ezekiel and Zechariah contain long apocalyptic segments. The most famous Old Testament apocalypse, the Book of Daniel, was written circa 165 B.C. The apocalyptic genre became more popular after 70 A.D., when the apocryphal apocalypses, 2 Baruch and 4 Ezra, were written in response to the destruction of the Jewish temple in Jerusalem by Roman armies. There is enough apocalyptic literature that it can be classified as a genre of its own, with its own particular characteristics. Some of these common features are revelations made to a human emissary through a supernatural agency, heavy symbolism, numerology with obscure significance, extravagant imagery, and concern about a cataclysmic day of judgment or the end of the world. Apocalyptic literature tends to take a deterministic view of history—that is, apocalypses are generally driven by the belief that history inexorably follows a set path ordained by God. All of these characteristics of the apocalyptic genre are present in Revelation.

SUMMARY

The introduction of Revelation names the author, John, and explains the immediacy of the message: the end of days is at hand. John extends a greeting to the Christian communities in seven major Near East cities in the name of the God of history. On the Sabbath, John falls into a prophetic ecstasy. He sees a vision of a shining Jesus, surrounded by seven stars and seven lamp-stands: these represent the seven churches of Asia. In 2:1–3:22, John is given orders to deliver a message to each of the churches, addressing specific strengths and failings of each church, providing encouragement to some and driving others to repent before Judgment Day. Jesus reminds them that his coming is imminent. The first half of John's revelatory experience begins with the opening of the heavenly door: "Come up here," a voice calls to him, "I will show you what is to take place in the future" (4:1). John sees God enthroned and surrounded by twenty-four elders.

Lightning flashes and thunder sounds. Old Testament angels with six wings and many eyes sing praises to the Lord. God holds a scroll sealed with seven seals, and nobody is worthy of breaking the seals except Jesus, by virtue of his sacrifice. Jesus appears here as "a Lamb standing as if it had been slaughtered," but also as "the Lion of the tribe of Judah" (5:5–6). Breaking the first four seals, Jesus releases the Four Horsemen of the Apocalypse: victory, war, famine, and pestilence. When the fifth seal is broken, the souls of martyrs cry out for justice, but they are urged to have patience until the appointed number of people have been martyred. The breaking of the sixth seal unleashes a massive cosmic upheaval that devastates the world.

Before the breaking of the seventh seal, an angel marks 144,000 people—12,000 from each of the tribes of Israel—with the seal of God to protect them from the coming devastation. Other righteous people, too, are to be saved: a "great multitude . . . [of people] from all the tribes and peoples and languages" have cleansed themselves and they, too, will be protected (7:9). Finally, it is time to open the seventh seal (8:1). But the opening of the seal is anti-climactic; when it is opened, it is revealed that there are seven trumpets that need to be blown. Four of the trumpets blow, each bringing with it disaster and destruction, with fire falling from the sky (8:6–12). With the fifth trumpet, the chimney leading out of the Abyss is unlocked, and bizarre locusts emerge in the smoke, stinging anyone unmarked by God's seal. The sixth trumpet unleashes a vast troop of cavalry who kill "a third of humankind" (9:18). However, the survivors nevertheless refuse to stop worshipping idols and behaving immorally. An angel descends from heaven, announcing the imminent fulfillment of "the mystery of God" with the blowing of the seventh trumpet (10:7).

The prophet is ordered to consume a scroll, which will taste sweet but be bitter in his stomach (8:10). He is told that two prophets will arise to preach the word of God in Jerusalem, but will be killed after 1,260 days by "the beast that comes up from the bottomless pit" (11:7). God will revive these prophets, and will strike Jerusalem with a powerful earthquake. Finally, the seventh trumpet blows, and John hears voices shouting, "The kingdom of the world has become the kingdom of our Lord and of his Messiah, and he will reign forever and ever" (11:15). The moment for justice, punishment, and triumph has arrived, with lighting, thunder, earthquakes, and hail.

The second half of Revelation begins with the opening of God's sanctuary in heaven. A woman "clothed with the sun, with the moon under her feet," gives birth to a child who is almost eaten by a huge red dragon with seven heads and ten horns (12:1). The child is saved from the dragon and brought to heaven. The archangel Michael makes war on the dragon, who is Satan, defeats him, and drives him from heaven. The dragon continues to pursue the woman, who yet again escapes him. Instead, he makes war on her children. The dragon delegates his power to a fantastical creature identified only as "the beast," who makes war on the saints and curses God (13:4). A false prophet, "another beast," arises and convinces people to worship the first beast (13:11). The prophet sees Jesus and his 144,000 righteous followers entrenched on Mount Zion in Jerusalem. He hears the news that the Day of Judgment is at hand, and that Babylon the Great—probably symbolic of the Roman Empire—has fallen. Angels begin to spill out of the blood of the wicked like wine from a winepress. While the righteous sing hymns to Moses and Jesus, seven angels empty seven bowls of plagues across the Earth, bringing suffering and destruction to the wicked. People refuse to repent, and instead curse God. With the pouring out of the seventh bowl, "it is done" (16:17).

John is shown a vision of the Whore of Babylon, who symbolizes the Roman Empire. An angel announces the fall of Babylon and warns God's faithful to abandon Rome, lest they be punished together with the wicked. Those wicked people who made their livings from Rome's trade will mourn her downfall, but the righteous will rejoice. Many voices surrounding the throne of God sing his praises at the news, and announce that the Lamb, Jesus, is soon to be wedded to his "bride," the faithful of God (19:7). John is ordered to write the wedding announcement: "Blessed are those who are invited to the wedding supper of the Lamb" (19:9). In the final battle, the gates of heaven open, and Jesus, clad now as a warrior named "Faithful and True," leads the hosts of heaven in a war against the beast and the kings of the Earth (19:11). The beast and his false prophet are hurled into a fiery lake, and the other opponents of Jesus are killed. Together with the saints, Jesus reigns for 1,000 glorious years. At the end of the 1,000 years, Satan gathers his forces, Gog and Magog, and again leads them into battle against the saints, but they are consumed by fire. Satan, too, is hurled into the fiery pit. On the Day of Judgment, which follows immediately, everyone is resurrected and judged "according to their works" (20:12). After Judgment Day, John sees a vision of "a new heaven and a new earth," and a new holy city of Jerusalem descended from heaven (21:1). The New Jerusalem is a picture of shining perfection, carved of precious stones and lit by the glory of God and Jesus, who are present in Jerusalem instead of a temple. John is commanded to publicize the vision that he has received: "Do not seal up the words of the prophesy of this book, for the time is near" (22:10). In the conclusion of Revelation, Jesus

himself promises that God will come soon to reward the righteous
and punish the wicked.

ANALYSIS

The Book of Revelation was probably written sometime between
81 and 89 A.D. by a man named John, in and around the cities in
Asia Minor. Some scholars contend that Revelation indeed talks
about the future, but it primarily seeks to understand the present, a
time that was almost certainly one of extreme stress for Christians.
Revelation itself indicates that John understood that a persecution
of Christians living in western Asia Minor was imminent, and
that the persecution would come from the Romans, who would
make demands for emperor worship that the Christians would
have to resist. John's revelation is an attempt to persuade the small
churches to turn away from imperial cult worship and toward the
true God, who was in charge of history and who will triumph in
the end. Revelation seeks to accommodate the contradiction of
the triumph of God in history with the continued oppressive rule
of the Romans.

Revelation's heavy use of imagination and provocative
symbolism is central to its rhetorical power. Revelation turns to
poetics and aesthetics to depict the imperial city of Rome as a beast,
stating that "its feet were like a bear's and its mouth was like a lion's
mouth" (13:2). The beast has ten horns and seven heads and carries
on its back "Babylon the great, mother of whores, and of the earth's
abominations" (17:5). Babylon, who is "drunk with the blood of
the saints and the blood of the witnesses to Jesus," represents the
Roman Empire (17:6). She is eventually judged by the more powerful God, who causes her fall in Revelation's climax: "He has judged
the great whore who corrupted the earth with her fornication, and

he has avenged on her the blood of his servants. . . . Fallen, fallen is Babylon the great!" (14:8, 19:2).

John's potent imagery is not only a "call for the endurance and faith of the saints" (13:10), but it also tries to move the audience to a decision to turn away from the beast "so that you do not take part in her sins" (18:4), and instead to turn toward the God of justice who "will wipe away every tear from their eyes" (21:4). Revelation persuades Christians to stake their lives on that decision. In Babylon, everything is for sale. John does not hedge about the immorality of such disparities between the rich and the poor. When Babylon is destroyed, neither God, Christ, the saints, the apostles, nor the prophets mourn. Those who are upset are "the merchants of the earth" (18:11) and "all whose trade is on the sea" (18:17). In addition, "the kings of the earth, who committed fornication and lived in luxury with her will weep and wail" (18:9).

Important Quotations Explained

1. But to what will I compare this generation? It is like children sitting in the marketplaces and calling to one another, "We played the flute for you, and you did not dance; we wailed, and you did not mourn." For John came neither eating nor drinking, and they say, "He has a demon," the Son of Man came eating and drinking, and they say, "Look, a glutton and a drunkard, a friend of tax collectors and sinners!" Yet wisdom is vindicated by her deeds. (Matthew 11:16–19)

Throughout the New Testament, there are references to Jesus as the wisdom of God, and here Matthew makes the association explicit. Wisdom in Jewish tradition bears a variety of meanings, but the most dominant role wisdom takes on is that of a teacher calling out to the public to take him in (Prov. 1:20–21, 9:3). This concept of wisdom correlates well with Matthew's overall definition of Christ's nature, which focuses on Jesus's role as a teacher, instructor, and sage (Matthew 11:1, 9:35).

In this parable, Jesus and John the Baptist can be interpreted to be the figures who call out from the marketplace, play the flute, dance, wail, and mourn. Those who will not join them are "this generation," which will not hear God's message. This interpretation is in keeping with the biblical figure of wisdom, which calls out to the public from marketplaces, crossroads, portals, and streets (Prov. 1:20–21, 8:1–3) and is met with similar rejection (Prov. 8:36–38). Wisdom says, "I have called and you refused, have stretched out my hand and no one heeded" (Prov. 1:24–25). Wisdom opens the community and widens participation. Jesus/Wisdom is justified by the deeds that recognize all Israelites as its children: "the blind receive their sight, the lame walk, the lepers are cleansed, the deaf hear, the dead are raised, and the poor have good news brought to them" (Matthew 4–5). While these deeds justify Jesus, they are the source of Jesus's rejection as a "glutton and a drunkard, friend of tax collectors and sinners" (Matthew 11:18).

2. In the beginning was the Word, and the Word was with God, and the Word was God. He was in the beginning with God. All things came into being through him, and without him not one thing came into being. What has come into being in him was life, and the life was the light of all people. The light that shines in the darkness, and the darkness did not overcome it. (John 1:1–5)

John's emphasis on Jesus as the Word of God incarnated is indebted both to Greek philosophy and to his Jewish heritage. The Greeks developed the concept of a divine force governing the balance between binary opposites in the universe. They called this force Logos, best translated as "Word" or "Reason." In many Greek conceptions, it is Logos that determines the balance between light and darkness, flesh and spirit. A world without Logos, the Greeks believed, would be chaos. The influence of the concept of the Logos was felt strongly by the Jewish sect knows as the Essenes, ascetics who believed that the world was shaped by struggles between opposing forces. John takes his philosophical inspiration, which manifests itself through his Christology and theology, from the Greeks via the Essenes. Jesus is the Word, the Logos, who is the instrument of total victory of light over darkness, its binary opposite: "What has come into being in him was life. And the life was the light of all people" (John 1:4). John's reference to the Essene and Greek systems of philosophy to explain Jesus's origin and significance is reflective of his Gospel's careful pedagogical style. More than the authors of the other Gospels, John is concerned with explaining significance rather than recording facts.

3. For in Christ Jesus you are all children of God through faith. As many of you as were baptized into Christ have clothed yourselves with Christ. There is no longer Jew or Greek, there is no longer slave or free, there is no longer male or female; for all of you are one in Christ Jesus. (Galatians 3:26–28)

The meaning of this passage, written by Paul in a letter to the church at Galatians, is still very much at the center of controversy among biblical scholars today. Some scholars contend that Paul's notion of equality here speaks of a spiritual or transcendental equality rather than a social equality. This interpretation diminishes the social implications of the texts. Others claim that Paul has in mind social or ecclesiastical equality with serious political implications. Biblical scholar Elisabeth Schüssler Fiorenza argues that among Christ's followers, status differences are no longer valid. Statements such as Paul's reflect an equality that many scholars claim was present in the vision and practice of the earliest Christian missionary movement. Currently, many feminist and other biblical scholars are reconstructing the early Christian community to find important traces of social egalitarianism. Many point to this passage as one of the most important indicators of the egalitarian ideals of the early Christian community.

4. A sower went out to sow his seed; and as he sowed, some fell on the path, and was trampled on, and the birds of the air ate it up. Some fell on the rock; and as it grew up, it withered for lack of moisture. Some fell among the thorns, and the thorns grew with it and choked it. Some fell into good soil and grew, and when it grew it produced a hundredfold. (Luke 8:5–8)

The parable of the sower is found in Matthew, Mark, and even some writings that are not in the Christian canon, such as the Gospel of Thomas. Because the parable is found in a relatively uniform manner in various places, and because scholars have concluded that Jesus spoke in parables, we can assume that this parable did in fact come from the historical figure of Jesus. The parable stresses the mystery of the unexpected acceptance of the Kingdom of God despite much failure in hearing, being heard, and understanding. In Mark's version of the parable (Mark 4:14–20), Jesus interprets the parable for his inner circle of followers, though most scholars conclude that such interpretations were later additions by the early church. Mark's allegorical interpretation reads the sower as the speaker of the good news, and the seed as the word with potential to take root and "bear fruit" (4:20). The path is interpreted as hearers who are vulnerable to various symbolic dangers. Birds represent the evil that takes away the work sowed in Christ's followers. Rocky ground represents hearers who eagerly accept the word with enthusiasm but eventually fall away. Thorns represent listeners who are consumed with secular matters. The good soil represents hearers who patiently accept the word and eventually bear fruit.

5. Now before the festival of the Passover, Jesus knew that his hour had come to depart from this world and go to the Father. Having loved his own who were in the world, he loved them to the end. [He] got up from the table, took off his outer robe, and tied a towel around himself. Then he poured water into a basin and began to wash the disciples' feet. . . . After he had washed their feet, had put on his robe, and had returned to the table, he said to them, ". . . I have set you an example, that you also should do as I have done to you. Very truly I tell you, servants are not greater than their master, nor are messengers greater than the one who sent them. If you know these things, you are blessed if you do them." (John 13:1, 4–5, 12–17)

Here, Jesus forms and participates in a community based on service and love to one another, setting an example to be followed by each of his disciples. For John's community, the purpose of the foot-cleansing here is not a ritual cleansing, such as Peter thinks, but the completion of Jesus's full revelation of service and love. Throughout John's Gospel, as this passage indicates, the exercise of leadership and power in the new ministry of Jesus is not one of ecclesiastical hierarchy, but one of love and service among a community of friends.

Review and Resources

Quiz

1. What does Simon Peter do for a living before he becomes an apostle?
    A.   He is a carpenter.
    B.   He is a fisherman.
    C.   He is an itinerant preacher.
    D.   He is a baker.

2. In the Gospel of Mark, how does the Virgin Mary learn of her pregnancy?
    A.   There is no virgin birth in the Gospel of Mark.
    B.   From the angel Gabriel
    C.   Joseph learns of the news in a dream.
    D.   Mary has a vision.

3. Who is Stephen in Acts of the Apostles?
    A.   Paul's intern
    B.   The first Christian martyr
    C.   The founder of the church at Corinth
    D.   One of the apostles

4. The author of Acts of the Apostles also wrote which of the four Gospels?
    A.   Matthew
    B.   Mark
    C.   Sebastian
    D.   Luke

5. According to the Gospel of Matthew, who visits Jesus at his birth and where does this meeting take place?
   A. The three wise men, in a stable
   B. Five shepherds, in a stable
   C. The three wise men, in a house
   D. Five shepherds, at a midwifery center in Palestine

6. By what name is Paul of Tarsus known before he begins his missionary activity?
   A. Simon
   B. Levi
   C. Saul
   D. Stephen

7. According to Paul's formulation in 1 Corinthians, which is the greatest of the imperishable qualities?
   A. Charity
   B. Chastity
   C. Hope
   D. Love

8. Who is the high priest of Jerusalem who put Jesus on trial?
   A. Caiaphas
   B. Pilate
   C. Herod
   D. Caesar

9. In the Gospel According to John, which of the apostles doubts Jesus's resurrection until he sees Jesus with his own eyes?
   A. Paul
   B. Thomas
   C. Judas
   D. Peter

10. In the Book of Revelation, who does the beast represent?
    A. Adulterous women
    B. The Roman Empire
    C. Nonbelievers
    D. Jesus when he returns

11. According to the Gospel of Matthew, where does Jesus's first public sermon take place?
    A. On the plain
    B. In Jerusalem
    C. In the temple
    D. On the mount

12. In the Gospel of John, for whom does Mary Magdalene mistake Jesus in his first resurrection appearance?
    A. Peter
    B. A gardener
    C. A ghost
    D. Her father

13. In Paul's letters to the Corinthians, what teaching is he trying to convey?
    A. Unity amidst diversity
    B. Sexual restraint
    C. Love as the most important virtue
    D. All of the above

14. How does Judas signal Jesus's identity to the Roman officials?
    A. He points to him.
    B. He kisses him.
    C. He hands them a drawing of him.
    D. He publicly pronounces Jesus's name.

15. Who discovers the empty tomb of Jesus?
    A. Peter
    B. Paul and Stephen
    C. Judas
    D. Mary Magdalene and Mary, mother of James and Joseph

16. Who murders John the Baptist?
    A. Herod the Great
    B. Ciaphas
    C. Pilate
    D. An angry mob

17. When Christians observe Palm Sunday, what biblical narrative are they celebrating?
    A. Jesus's feeding of the 5,000
    B. The Last Supper
    C. Jesus's entry into Jerusalem before his death
    D. The Sermon on the Mount

18. According to the Gospels, what is the unique literary genre Jesus employs to preach his message?
    A. The parable
    B. Mystery sayings
    C. Comic-tragic drama
    D. Proverbial sayings

19. Which Gospel is most concerned with the mystery and identity of the person of Jesus?
    A. Matthew
    B. John
    C. Mark
    D. James

20. Who baptizes Jesus?
    A. Mary
    B. Joseph
    C. John the Baptist
    D. Herod

21.   Who takes Jesus's body off the cross?
    A.   Joseph of Arimathea
    B.   Peter
    C.   Mary
    D.   Martha

22.   Who is the first apostle to deny Jesus?
    A.   Judas
    B.   Peter
    C.   Mary
    D.   Lazarus

23.   Which part of the New Testament is written by Jesus?
    A.   The Gospels
    B.   Revelation
    C.   Nothing in the New Testament is written by Jesus.
    D.   Acts

24.   When was the New Testament written?
    A.   While Jesus was preaching and traveling
    B.   Between 70 and 120 A.D.
    C.   300 A.D.
    D.   35 A.D.

ANSWER KEY
1: B; 2: A; 3: B; 4: D; 5: C; 6: C; 7: D; 8: A; 9: B; 10: B; 11: D; 12: B;
13: D; 14: B; 15: D; 16: A; 17: C; 18: A; 19: B; 20: C; 21: A; 22: A;
23: C; 24: B; 25: C

FURTHER READING

DULING, DENNIS C., and NORMAN PERRIN. *The New Testament: Proclamation and Parenesis, Myth and History.* New York: Harcourt College Publishers, 1994.

FELDER, CAIN HOPE. *Stony the Road We Trod: African American Biblical Interpretation.* Minneapolis: Fortress Press, 1991.

FREEDMAN, DAVID NOEL, ed. *The Anchor Bible Dictionary.* New York: Doubleday, 1998.

FIORENZA, ELISABETH SCHÜSSLER. *In Memory of Her: A Feminist Theological Reconstruction of Christian Origins.* New York: Crossroad Publishing Company, 10th Anniversary Edition, 1994.

HARRISVILLE, ROY A., and WALTER SUNDBERG. *Baruch Spinoza to Brevard Childs.* Grand Rapids, MI: Eerdmans Publishing, 2nd edition, 2002.

MCDONALD, LEE M. *The Formation of the Christian Biblical Canon.* Peabody, MA: Hendrickson Publishers, 1995.

THEISSEN, GERD. *The Social Setting of Pauline Christianity: Essays on Corinth.* Edited and translated by John H. Schütz. Philadelphia: Fortress Press, 1982.